Momma, Don't Hit Me!

A True Story of Child Abuse

By Shannon Bowen

Fourth Edition

NEW FOREST
BOOKS

Author's statement: I have tried to recreate events, locales and conversations from my memories of them. In order to maintain their anonymity in some instances I have changed the names of individuals and places, I may have changed some identifying characteristics and details such as physical properties, occupations and places of residence.

To contact the author, visit Shannon-Bowen.com.

Other books by Shannon Bowen:
- Momma, Stop! I'll Be Good!
- What Happened to Kevin - Two-book set (combining both "Momma" books)
- The Wicked Widow (co-author)

ISBN 978-1522910275

Fourth edition, published December 2015 by New Forest Books, Concord, NH and Orlando, FL.

Table of Contents

Introduction

This isn't a novel. It's a real-life, "warts and all" diary about living next door to a child abuser for over a year.

I regularly wrote in this portion of my diary from the middle of June 2012 to October 2012. I didn't expect to publish it. Frankly, this story isn't entertaining... but it is true.

Also, I didn't keep notes during the early months. I kept thinking the landlord, police, and Child Services offices would intervene quickly. During that time, I called and visited the police station. I called and visited our apartment manager's office. I called the NH state office for Child Protective Services.

Those efforts weren't part of my diary, and had to be reconstructed later, when I decided to use this book to bring attention to Kevin's plight.

People have asked why I didn't do more. Well, I did everything I could, within the law. The manager's and landlord's rights and responsibilities were limited, and they had concerns about liability issues. The police could only act on something tangible — abuse they'd witnessed themselves, or that a large number of credible witnesses said they'd seen occur. The state offices are underfunded and overworked, and unable to investigate every case that's reported. And, due to privacy laws, the state cannot adequately oversee staff and funding issues at offices assigned to handle abuse cases.

This part of the story *is* complete, but it's actually the first part of a two-part story. At the time I first published this, I thought Kevin's troubles were over, and the end of this book was the "happily ever after" end to the story.

I was wrong.

If you've wondered why child abuse isn't reported or resolved as quickly as it should be, this book will show you what *really* happens when neighbors try to help an abused child and his out-of-control, struggling family.

Though the abuse and neglected happened, over and over again, there was no simple way to help Kevin.

Each individual who could have helped either couldn't do anything without... well, *something* more, like a broken bone or Kevin admitting that he was terrified of his mother. Or, they looked the other way.

The events I describe are real, though I've changed names and identifying details. I've also included some events not involving Kevin. I wanted to give you a better picture of the kinds of people who live and visit here, and why I was often the lone voice trying to get help for Kevin: The neighbors already knew it was futile.

I believe my diary tells a compelling story of child abuse and neglect, and the broken systems that fail our society and the children who desperately need our help.

Who's Who

In this book, the people I talked about most were our next-door neighbors between October 2011 and early 2013. I've changed some personal details about the adults to protect their privacy and my own.

Kevin was a preschool child whose bedroom was on the other side of the wall from mine. He was three years old when he and his parents moved into apartment next to ours.

Ann was his mother, whose life of excess seemed certain to lead to disaster.

Joe was Kevin's father, a factory worker and former high school football star.

Maryann was the apartment manager, and my only consistent supporter as we tried to get help for Kevin.

Alphabetical list with more details

Ann was Kevin's mother. I think she's a high school dropout and, when she lived next to me, she was in her early 20s but looked much older. She appeared to be increasingly involved with drugs and prostitution.

Denise was a quiet woman and a friend of Ann and Joe. She often provided transportation for Ann, who didn't seem to drive. When Denise spent the night — for what usually looked like a threesome — Ann seemed to treat Kevin better.

Erik was the head of maintenance at our apartment complex. He's a bright, funny guy. He's married to Maryann, who was the manager of our apartment complex and the adjoining condos.

Handshake King (HK) was a cryptic young man who was part of the story — and perhaps a catalyst — during the summer of 2012. When he was here, I wasn't sure if he was an undercover police officer, a drug dealer, or neither. He was an enigma when he was here, and left a lasting impact on the community.

Henry was a regular visitor, next door. He looked about 16 years old. For about a month, he was also Kevin's live-in babysitter. Henry seemed to have a crush on Ann, despite how she treated him. He'd been thrown out of his home when his new stepmother arrived.

Joe was Kevin's father. During this part of the story, Joe seemed like a quiet man. He was in his early 20s, with a background in sports. He worked at the same factory as his dad did. Most of the time, he seemed very nice, but a little too worn-down by life. Later, things changed. Even now, after all that happened, I hope I was completely wrong about him. I hope he recovers his high school dreams, cut short by Ann's pregnancy and his own internal demons.

Kevin was the child. He was three years old in October 2011, when this story started. When he lived next to us, he seemed bright and almost sweet at times. However, most of the time, he was a loud, out-of-control child with behavior issue. Given his home life, that's no surprise.

Maryann was the apartment manager, and a mom herself. She was always cheerful, but — underneath the sunny smile — I'm pretty sure she's a shrewd judge of character. I liked her, and she was a tremendous sounding board when I felt that no one else was listening. Without her support, I'm not sure that I'd have remained such a strong advocate for Kevin's safety. She encouraged me every step of the way, when -- due to liability issues -- she was unable to step in and do anything, herself.

Pippi was a downstairs neighbor and single mom in her 20s. She was an on-again, off-again friend for Ann, and — during this same time period — Pippi went through a lot of drama in her own life.

That turbulence was far more visible to our neighbors than what was going on in Kevin's apartment.

I was Kevin's neighbor. I'm happily married to Pete. When we lived next door to Kevin, Pete worked second shift at his office, so he witnessed some things that I didn't, and vice versa. Pete and I have three children. I write travel articles and books under a pen name.

The Diary Entries

Nov 2011 – First Warnings and Confusion

We live in a mid-size apartment complex in New Hampshire, about 20 minutes from one of the state's larger cities. (However, no city in New Hampshire is "large" compared with NYC, Los Angeles, Houston, Chicago, or London.) People merely stop here for food or gas, on their way to one of New Hampshire's many vacation spots.

Most of our neighbors are working class. About half are single, and most are in their 20s, 30s, or 40s. They like motorcycles and snowmobiles, and enjoy Little League games with their kids. Adults with jobs are usually employed by local chain restaurants or they work in a "big box" or outlet store.

For entertainment, our neighbors go to the pizza place, the diner, a bar, a friend's barbecue, or to tractor pulls. Our public library is in the same little brick building that's housed it since the 1800s. We're within 30 minutes of a popular outlet mall, and — like many New Hampshire towns — the homemade ice cream stand is one of the most popular summer hangouts.

In other words, this is a typical New Hampshire town.

One Saturday morning, early in November 2011, I visited the apartment manager's office. Instead of the manager, I met the landlord for the first time in over three years.

He seemed like a nice man, but I was uncomfortable explaining why I was there. I was about to accuse a new neighbor of child abuse.

About ten days earlier, a young family — Joe, Ann, and their three-year-old son, Kevin — had moved in, next door to us.

I told our landlord that, on the previous night, I'd heard what sounded like Joe beating his son.

I'd been woken in the middle of the night by the sound of someone or something hitting the wall, repeatedly. I also heard what sounded like punches, or skin hitting skin.

I heard Kevin, the three-year-old next door, shout something that sounded like "Daddy, stop, Daddy, please, Daddy, stop!"

This went on for at least 15 – 20 minutes, maybe longer. (I'm not sure *how* slowly I woke up after the assault started. Ordinarily, I'm a sound sleeper.)

Then it stopped. I had trouble falling asleep again. The experience was really upsetting.

It was also completely unexpected.

Shortly after the family moved in, I'd met Ann. I'd been impressed by how nice she seemed. She told me that she was working three jobs *and* going to school to complete her degree. She seemed polite, well-spoken, and very caring. On Halloween night, everyone seemed to know and like her. She called people by name and asked about their families. I thought she was an ideal neighbor.

By contrast, Joe seemed very subdued. He looked at the ground most of the time, and he rarely replied when my husband and I said hello.

Joe is a big guy. He clenches and relaxes his fists, repeatedly, as he walks. His knuckles are often pinker than I'd expect. So, I assumed that Joe was responsible for the violence.

Also, what Kevin shouted and screamed *seemed* to confirm those first impressions. I was about 90% certain that I'd heard Joe beating his son.

The landlord told me to call the apartment manager, day or night, if I heard it again. He assured me that they'd act as a buffer between neighbors and me. The landlord wanted to avoid direct confrontations between tenants.

I liked that.

But then, the landlord said the apartment manager would call the police. That made me uneasy. I didn't want to report Joe (Kevin's father) *until I was absolutely certain he was abusing his son.*

Shortly after that, I guess Joe got the message that I could hear Kevin hitting the wall.

Joe knocked on my door, apologized, and said he'd move Kevin's bed to another part of the room where I was less likely to be disturbed. He also promised to swap bedrooms with Kevin, if the little boy continued hitting the wall at night.

Joe seemed very nice. I wanted to like him, but — after that conversation — he stopped looking at me. He *never* said hello when we passed each other in the hallway or in the parking lot. He tilted his head so I couldn't see much of his face.

He wasn't just ignoring me. He was *avoiding* me. That made me uneasy.

For the next couple of weeks, everything seemed quiet in Kevin's apartment.

But then the hitting noises, shouting and crying started again. They always occurred after 10 PM. I'm pretty sure they woke me up once every couple of weeks, but I wasn't keeping a diary at that point.

I didn't call the manager, yet. After all, it was the middle of the night (I hate to wake up *anyone*), and I wasn't *entirely* certain the dad was responsible.

I could hear Kevin screaming, and thuds that sounded like physical assaults, but I wasn't absolutely *certain* what was going on or which adult I heard. The voice was too low to be sure.

Also, Ann had warned me that Kevin was

having difficulty settling into apartment living. She'd explained that he might be a little noisy at times. She was doing her best to be a good mom, along with her jobs and college courses. She'd apologized and said it might be a few weeks until she could get Kevin to settle down.

So, it seemed reasonable that a parent was trying to get Kevin to stay in bed, and *Kevin* was the one doing the hitting, not a parent.

(I can still recall nights when my own kids wanted to stay up past their bedtimes. Sometimes, I'd have to pick them up and put them to bed while they shouted and hit me. That didn't happen very often, but it *could* explain the noises I heard from Kevin's bedroom.)

I wanted to believe that Kevin — three years old at the time — wasn't being abused, and I'd misinterpreted what I'd heard.

So, I said nothing and kept listening, trying to figure out what was *really* going on.

Jan 2012 – Kevin Thrown Out

Late in January 2012 — I think it was Thursday, January 26th — Kevin was running around the apartment, making noise. He was making the normal, loud sounds of a boy running around and playing.

I was in my home office, working, so I did my best to ignore his shouting and occasional thumps on the wall. I think he was being a Power Ranger. It was one of his favorite games.

Then, around 3 PM, I heard an apartment door open, hard. It sounded as if it had been slammed against the nearby wall. After that, I heard loud arguing, so I went to my living room to find out what was going on.

Through the security window in my door, I

could see Ann and Kevin just inside their apartment. The door was open. Kevin was fussing and whining.

Ann — Kevin's mother — pushed him into the hall and shouted at him, "If you're going to act like that, you can just stay out until tomorrow."

It was a harsh, deep voice. Until now, I'd never heard Ann use that voice... not when I was sure it was her, anyway.

Then, Ann slammed the door and locked it, loudly, so the little boy couldn't get back in.

The odd thing was: Kevin stopped fussing. He looked around for a few seconds, and then sat down on the top step. His little knees were together. He had one hand in his lap, and the other on the railing. His tiny fingers tapped thoughtfully as if he were playing the piano. He seemed entirely calm and contented.

It wasn't a reaction I'd expected.

I peeked out my door a few minutes later, to see what was going on. Kevin was still seated on the stairs and he seemed very happy out there.

After about 20 minutes, Ann threw open the door and told Kevin to "get [his] butt in" the apartment. Her voice was loud and ugly. Kevin didn't say anything, but I heard the apartment door close. That's when Kevin started fussing again, inside the apartment. It wasn't loud crying, but he was very unhappy.

At other times during the winter, Ann seemed to shut Kevin out of the apartment. However, Kevin's dad usually came home soon afterward. Maybe Kevin was just waiting eagerly for his dad to return, and Ann allowed him to wait on the stairs.

That's what I preferred to believe, but I'd never leave a three-year-old unsupervised outside an apartment. Not at the top of a long flight of stairs.

All in all, Ann's behavior was increasingly strange. Every time I saw or heard her, she seemed less like the bright, cheerful woman she was when she'd first moved in. Was she still working three jobs *and* going to college? If so, she was tip-toeing in and out of the apartment. I never saw her leave or return home.

However, Joe left and returned daily, like clockwork. He worked the 7-to-3 shift at the local factory. I figured his income was enough to allow Ann to stay home with Kevin, and continue her studies, online. That's how I explained what was going on, anyway.

Still, something seemed *odd*. I couldn't put my finger on it.

During January, Kevin's thuds, thumps, and crying occurred less frequently. Late at night, maybe Kevin *was* putting up a fight after getting out of bed. I wasn't certain. However, it felt like one of those "calm before the storm" situations.

Nov – Apr: Additional Info

From November 2011 through April 2012, I heard Kevin shouting and screaming about once every week or 10 days. It might have been far more often, but — as I write this — I want to err on the side of caution. I don't want to describe this as something worse than it is.

Some weeks were awful. After that, everything would be fine for a couple of weeks. The *awful* weeks seemed to be growing worse. But, on average, I could expect a loud nighttime scene in Kevin's bedroom once a week or so.

For the first couple of months, the adult's voice was too quiet to identify. I couldn't even tell if it was male or female. Kevin usually begged, "Daddy, please!" I heard that repeatedly.

Also, I never heard anything that I was *sure* was physical abuse. I didn't want to report anything unless I was more certain about what was going on, and who was involved. However, after the first couple of weeks, I did call the apartment manager, Maryann, each time I heard alarming noises from Kevin's bedroom for more than a few minutes. I assumed she was passing this information to the police and the landlord.

As time went on, the adult's voice sounded *more* like Ann's low-pitched, ugly voice... the one I'd heard when she threw Kevin out of the apartment. However, since I'd only heard Joe's voice once — when he apologized for the noise against my bedroom wall — I couldn't be sure.

During that time, I saw Ann only once. It was when we were both in the hallway. She apologized again for how noisy Kevin was. She said he was *still* getting used to apartment living. Her in-laws had allowed Kevin to be very noisy in their home. That's one reason why she'd wanted to move out of their house.

She promised that she was working on the problem, but she wasn't getting much help from her partner. He kept Kevin up too late at night. Then, when Ann got home from work, it was difficult to get Kevin to settle down.

Ann explained that she had a new — and exhausting — job as a waitress. She asked for my patience. She knew Kevin's noises were unacceptable, but she didn't have a quick solution.

Many evenings, I often heard Kevin and his dad playing when Ann wasn't at home. I heard shouting and running, but I always heard lots of laughing, too. Normal stuff. Usually, it sounded like Kevin went to bed by 8 or 9 PM.

So, Ann's version of the story didn't ring true.

I *wanted* to be understanding about Ann's

15

dilemma. As she explained it, she had to be the disciplinarian. Joe didn't provide much help. However, each time I heard Kevin screaming and crying, I was more certain the adult's voice was Ann's.

After Ann began spending most of her time at home, I also heard Kevin screaming and crying when Joe *wasn't* at home.

I called DHHS (the New Hampshire office where child abuse and family issues are reported), to ask their advice. I thought they might visit and interview Kevin's family to get to the heart of the issue.

The caseworker already had a file about Kevin, probably from Maryann's reports. I probably should have expected that.

The caseworker surprised me even more when she said that Ann and Joe were in their early 20s. Both looked in their 30s. The caseworker said that's not unusual. She explained that people on drugs often look far older than they are. Since I hadn't mentioned drugs — or even thought about Ann and Joe using them — I didn't know how to respond.

The caseworker said she could send someone out to evaluate what sounded like *neglect*. However, DHHS needed more evidence, including police reports, to look into physical *abuse*.

I continued to call Maryann when I heard Kevin screaming. I began calling the police myself, as well.

The following is edited from one of my reports to the police. This was what I said in March 2012:

"The pattern was consistent. I'd hear Ann storming up the stairs. That's what usually woke me up: Her heavy footsteps. Sometimes, she'd also slam the front door, loudly.

"A few minutes later, I'd hear Kevin's door hit the wall. Then I'd hear Kevin whimper, followed by angry words (rarely clear enough to understand) from Ann. Then, Kevin would sound fully awake and start shouting for his father.

"I'd also hear something hitting the wall, usually five or six times. I assumed it was Kevin kicking the wall or throwing shoes against the wall. That's what it sounded like, or what I wanted to believe it was.

"Ann's low, angry voice and Kevin's shouting would continue for 15 – 20 minutes, with lots of thuds and thumps. It always ended very abruptly with one final thud followed by complete silence. Maybe Kevin ran out of things to throw."

I know that sounds very conservative, but I didn't want to accuse Ann of a crime she might not have committed.

March 2012

During March 2012, things turned worse. Bill collectors knocked at Ann's door every few days, demanding payment.

The two times I clearly heard Ann's replies, she said (loudly) that her husband promised he was dropping off the payment that day. Each time, Ann said she'd call Joe at work to be sure he'd make the payment on his way home from work.

That's when I started hearing shouting and thuds in the bathroom, usually late in the day. I figured Ann was having a difficult time getting Kevin to take a bath. Sometimes, it sounded as if someone had slipped in the tub, or something heavy had fallen off the bathroom counter.

Also, the late-night crying and shouting episodes became more frequent, sometimes two or three times a week. After about 15 or 20 minutes, the voices faded. I think Ann took Kevin to another part of the apartment.

One night, Ann opened the door to the hall, stood in the doorway, and shouted at her partner that he had been treating her like [waste matter] and, from now on, she was going to treat him the same way. It seemed as if Ann wanted the whole building to hear her.

Ann seemed out of control, and I didn't know how to help her or her family.

April 2012

In late April 2012, I realized the authorities weren't doing anything, nor was the apartment owner. I understood that Maryann wanted to keep out of it. That's against the law — in NH, you're required to report any and all suspected child abuse — but she knew I was reporting it. I'm pretty sure Maryann was (unofficially) talking to at least one of our town's police officers about the problem.

I decided to keep a regular diary of what was going on at Kevin's apartment. The fact that DHHS already had a file about him... that surprised and worried me. So far, calling the apartment manager, the police, and DHHS hadn't helped Kevin and his family.

Now I wanted everything written down, at least in a blog, so I had a clearer picture of what I was witnessing.

In my first April entries, I did not include my calls to the police. When I'd first kept my diary, I didn't expect anyone except the police and DHHS to need my information, and they already had records of my calls for help.

Monday, April 23rd

During the night, I witnessed the usual routine, but with a few variations *and* it went on longer than usual.

Keep in mind: These noises were loud enough to hear *through the wall,* and over the noise of three electric fans. We deliberately keep fans running, 24/7, to minimize how much we hear from Kevin's apartment and other occasionally noisy neighbors.

On Monday night, I had been asleep for about three hours. Noises from next door woke me from a sound sleep.

Here's what happened:

1. Ann came home, a little before midnight.

2. I heard Kevin's bedroom door open, hitting the wall, and then slam closed.

3. I heard Kevin shouting. His voice sounded as if he was scared and protesting.

4. I heard Ann's voice, loud but in her "nice" voice... the one she uses *outside* the apartment. It seemed completely inconsistent with Kevin's shouts for his father.

5. I heard a few thuds and thumps that sounded different from when Kevin is kicking the wall or throwing things. Kevin kept shouting and Ann kept talking. This went on for about 15 minutes.

6. Suddenly, Kevin was completely quiet.

About 15 minutes later, I heard Kevin's door open again. This time, Ann's voice *wasn't* her public voice. It was the one that's low, ragged-sounding, and harsh. When she uses that voice, her words seem to run together. I can barely understand them at all.

I heard more thuds, as if someone was hitting (or being hit by) a heavy object.

Kevin screamed things like "Help! Daddy! Please! Daddy!", repeatedly. His voice was clear.

At that point, Ann's voice was so low and muffled, I couldn't understand a word. (That's normal. Usually, the *only* time I can understand their words is when Kevin is screaming, or Ann is standing near their front door.)

Suddenly, after about 15 or 20 minutes, Kevin was quiet. The thuds stopped, and I heard his bedroom door slam.

Everything was quiet for another hour or so. Then, the sequence began again. This repeated several times, until around three in the morning.

Either the violence stopped or I was so exhausted, I didn't wake up for later episodes.

Tuesday, April 24th

On this date, around 3:20 PM and continuing for at least 20 minutes, I heard something that sounded like a padded chair or a body hitting the apartment wall, repeatedly but not rhythmically.

In other words, Kevin hadn't developed superhuman strength. He wasn't suddenly throwing furniture instead of a ball or his toys.

During that time, I heard Ann's angry voice and Kevin shouting, crying, and occasionally screaming. Both voices came from the same part of the room where the wall was being hit. It's the wall that adjoins my bedroom.

The sounds were *awful*, and the worst to date.

Ann's various voices worried me, too. It's sounding like more than the difference between an act she puts on in public, and her private voice. The vocabulary didn't vary that much, when I could hear her clearly through her front door, but the changing tone of voice seemed far *more* than just social v. relaxed.

I ran to the police station and told them what was going on, in person. Then I went to Maryann's office to tell her what was going on.

Here's the really strange thing:

Maryann called Joe so he'd stop in on his way home from work.

While we waited for him, Maryann called Joe's mother. During that phone call, I also explained the situation to Joe's mother. She said she'd look for bruising to report to DHHS.

When Joe arrived, Maryann asked me to tell him what I've heard from Kevin's bedroom and when Joe isn't at home.

I described the situation in detail.

Joe didn't blink. He insisted he's a sound sleeper. He said he's never heard Kevin in trouble or Ann abusing Kevin.

Joe didn't challenge me at all. He didn't ask for details. He didn't ask me if I was *sure* it was Ann, *sure* it was abuse, or anything like that. He just looked at me, almost impatiently.

He said he's in the process of filing for full custody. I heard no emotion in his voice.

Then he said he had to get back to the apartment because Ann would notice he wasn't there.

As a former Girl Scout Leader and camp director, I've had this kind of conversation before. Thank heavens, it's been rare. However, in my experience, the innocent parent *always* wants to believe that it's just a misunderstanding.

Even when you can see, in their eyes, that *they'd suspected something...* they *still* ask questions. They just *don't want to believe* that someone is hurting their child. They resist the idea that the other parent (or another family member) is the abuser.

It doesn't matter if the couple are on the verge

of divorce. It doesn't matter if they hate each other. There's almost always an effort to find a *different* explanation for what's going on. Nobody wants to believe that child abuse is going on, right under his nose.

However, Joe looked at me as if I'd told him the color of his car, or something else perfectly routine. He didn't look surprised. He didn't look upset. If anything, he looked *bored*.

Maybe it's a cultural thing. I'm not from this area.

Maybe it's the age difference; maybe 20-something parents are more accustomed to stories of abuse.

Maybe he's being abused as well, and I was seeing "frozen features."

Or, maybe Joe's reaction was simply guarded.

Monday, April 30th

The conversation with Joe continued to bother me. How could he *not* know what was going on in the bedroom next to his?

I wanted to believe Ann was beating Kevin only on nights when Joe wasn't at home.

Then, one night when Ann's shouting and Kevin's screams were especially bad, I checked the parking lot. I wanted to see if Joe's car was there.

It was.

To this day, Joe's mother insists that Joe has always been a sound sleeper. Maybe he is.

Still, I was pretty sure I heard another neighbor pounding on the wall or floor, and shouting at Ann to quiet down.

If the noise is loud enough to wake the neighbors, how is Joe sleeping through it? He might be awake *and* aware of what's going on in Kevin's bedroom. Maybe Joe is also a victim of

Ann's abuse and doesn't want to admit it.

Anyway, by the time I'd looked out to see Joe's car in the parking lot, it sounded as if Ann had moved to the living room with Kevin. After several loud thumps, I heard Ann shout at Kevin, "No, I did not hit you with a toy," and then, "Get your ass into bed."

I was dialing the phone — calling the police — when everything went silent next door, so I stopped dialing. I didn't hear anything after that.

Before I make further calls to the police, I'll talk with the apartment manager. Maybe she understands this better than I do. I want to be *very* sure I know what's going on and how broad the responsibility must be.

Something doesn't add up. The key to the puzzle might be Joe's role in this.

May 2011

In May, I went back to our apartment manager's office. Nothing had changed at Kevin's apartment. If anything, the abuse was getting worse.

Here's what I wrote in my dairy:

It's clear that Ann *isn't* just struggling with problems created by too-lenient grandparents. Kevin isn't just "getting used to apartment living." If he were, his behavior would have improved over the past six months.

I believe that Ann is the abuser, and Joe is looking the other way. I'm not sure why he'd do that. Kevin is his *son*, for heaven's sake.

So, tired of losing sleep over this, and not sure what to do next, I visited the apartment manager's office.

Maryann (the apartment manager) explained that Joe (Kevin's father) couldn't do anything about custody, yet. I'm not *sure,* but it sounds like — a year ago — Ann had filed domestic abuse charges against Joe, and Joe is in a court-ordered anger management program.

Until Joe completes that program, Maryann says there's no way he can get custody of his son. Well, that's what Joe told her, anyway.

I explained that I couldn't continue to listen to that kind of abuse.

Maryann told me to call the police in the future, not her. She said she's done everything she can.

I wasn't happy about that.

Ann radically changes her appearance and uses different voices. In the past, she used her inside-the-apartment voice or her public voice. Now she uses at least *three* distinctly different voices.

I'm worried. Ann might have multiple personalities or dissociative issues. Maybe drugs significantly alter her personality. I don't want to deal with those possibilities.

The police have warned me to avoid contact with Ann and Joe. The police say they need *different* evidence to protect Kevin. They *know* something's going on in that apartment, but the ways the laws are written... the police can't do anything, yet.

Just *hearing* shouting and hitting through Ann's door... the police can't do anything with that. Ann always has a quick explanation. The police need to *witness* physical abuse.

Meanwhile, they don't want me or my family to become casualties.

I don't know what their plan is. How do the police expect to *see* something *that only goes on behind closed doors?*

This makes no sense, but I'm following their advice.

Meanwhile, I am worried. An abuse parent is bad enough. Dissociative issues are *different* and can be more dangerous for me and my family. By now, I'm sure it's obvious to Ann that I'm the one calling the police. That makes me a potential target for her anger, as well.

I've tried to help Kevin. I've called the police. I've called DHHS. I've filed reports. Nothing seems to happen. Nothing seems to change. There are days when I wonder: Do they think I'm making this up, or what? Why can't *anyone* help Kevin?

The lack of sleep is catching up with me.

Recently, another neighbor complained about the smell of marijuana around Ann's apartment. If I'd smelled anything, I'd probably think it was incense and ignore it. Maryann said another neighbor thought she saw Ann buying drugs in the apartment parking lot.

Looking for a quick, simple answer, I'd *like* to blame all of this on drugs, but I can't be sure. And really, *does it matter?* The issue is a child at risk.

Meanwhile, I think Ann deliberately changes personalities like a chameleon, based on the impression she wants to make. Maybe she has three or five "outside" voices she draws on for different social settings. Inside her apartment, when she thinks no one is listening, she drops her guard. Maybe her *real* voice is the grating, unpleasant voice that I often hear.

But maybe — due to lack of sleep — I'm being too anxious. The focus *must* be on Kevin's safety. With him out of risk, Ann's issues can be addressed separately, with the help of her family.

Maryann said the police were looking for bruises or any marks on Kevin. They need physical proof that he's being hurt. So, until that's obvious, nothing is likely to change. I think Maryann is pretty fed up with this situation. Ann isn't the only troublesome tenant in this complex.

I'll be more watchful, but Kevin is so rarely outside the apartment — and the hallway lighting is so yellowish anyway — I'm not sure I'd see more than normal bruising that almost every active child has.

Thursday, June 14th

After 9:30 AM, Kevin was more active and noisy than usual. They were normal noises a boisterous boy makes, playing with toys, but they *were* louder than usual.

Shortly after 10 AM, I heard heavy footsteps. Then Kevin said loudly, "No, Mommy, no!"

Ann's shouted, "I'm going to hit you so hard!"

Immediately after that, I heard Kevin's voice or something like it. There were no words, just a noise like an animal. Next, I heard a very loud thud. It didn't sound like a toy had hit the wall, or like Kevin was punching the wall or kicking it. It sounded like a heavy thud like a body or a padded chair hitting the wall.

Finally, I heard Kevin's voice again, whimpering quietly, and — within a minute — everything was completely quiet.

Monday, June 18th

I've decided to make this a regular diary, so I record *everything* that might be important, as it happens. Maybe DHHS will listen to me if I have more details like dates and exact times. Or, maybe Joe can use this information to get full custody.

And, from a completely selfish point of view, venting in this diary helps me get back in focus. By putting these events on (virtual) paper, I can put a period to the end of each interruption and get back to work. If I can't help Kevin and his family, I need to earn enough to move my own family away from this.

So, anyway...

This morning, Ann knocked on my door. She was smiling and made lots of eye contact. She needed to borrow a can opener. She said that Joe must have thrown hers out.

(I'm sure the smile froze on my face. Ann never misses an opportunity to blame Joe for... well, anything and everything. That's fine when it's earned, but expecting me to believe Joe *threw out* a can opener — or that I'd even *care* — is a bit much.)

Ann was wearing a tank top. On the insides of her arms, I thought I saw weird bruises. Then, I realized they looked like temporary tattoos. The thing was, they were in the weirdest places on her arm... no rhyme or reason to the array. At a couple of them, I saw pinkish smudges like lipstick or insect bites.

Maybe Ann and Kevin were playing, and he put the designs on her with markers. That seemed unlikely, but I've never seen anything like them. For all I know, they were tattoos with specific meanings for Ann.

Anyway, I was pretty sure I'd been staring at Ann's arms. That was rude. I felt embarrassed.

I went to my kitchen and returned with our can opener. Again, Ann made eye contact. She took the can opener, thanked me, and promised to bring it right back.

A few minutes later, she returned with it. She thanked me again, almost going out of her way to make eye contact. She handed me the can opener and went back to her apartment.

About 20 minutes later, I talked with my husband. I said I'd been planning to buy a new can opener anyway, so why not give the old one to Ann?

My husband agreed, so I washed the can opener, dried it, and carried it to Ann's door. I knocked, but no one answered.

I waited, and knocked again.

Finally, Kevin opened the door. As usual, he was wearing underpants and that's all.

I asked him if his mother was around. Kevin pointed toward the bathroom, and visibly squirmed. He said he can't bother his mom when she's in the bathroom. (Well, hey, we *all* need time alone, now and then. Maybe the bathroom is her only refuge.)

I waited, and noticed Henry on the sofa, with his back to me. (Henry is teenager and a regular visitor at Ann's. I think he's Kevin's babysitter.)

I said, "I'd like to give this can opener to Ann, so she has one." Henry said he was busy, applying online for a job. He didn't look at me.

I waited. Feeling very uncomfortable, I finally handed the can opener to Kevin and told him to give it to his mom.

At that point, Ann emerged from the bathroom. No toilet flush. No sound of running water.

Her color was kind of pasty. She was definitely *avoiding* eye contact.

Kevin handed the can opener back to me, and I passed it to Ann.

I explained that I'd like her to keep the can opener since I'd been planning to buy a new one, anyway.

She muttered, "Sure," and — still not looking at me — she closed the door as I stepped back into the hallway. Nothing resembling thanks. (I didn't really expect any. I don't do nice things for *thanks*... I do them because that's the right thing to do.)

Maybe nothing odd was going on. Maybe Ann was fighting off an IBS episode or something. Her coloring looked pale and clammy, and her eyes seemed kind of glassy... what I could see of them, anyway. And, maybe she was glancing everywhere *except* at me because she wanted me to *leave*. Still, it was odd enough to note here.

Thursday, June 21st

Nightly noises continued in Kevin's bedroom. Some sounded like abuse, but they were so brief, I didn't have time to call the police.

Today, I had *another* odd conversation with Ann.

Around noon, Ann knocked on my door again. (This was a few days after the strange can opener conversations.)

This time, on a day with record-breaking heat in the 90s, Ann was wearing a heavy, long-sleeve hoodie with the hood up. Maybe she wanted to conceal the odd tattoos I'd stared at.

Kevin was in her arms. As usual, he was wearing underpants and nothing else. In that heat, it was a prudent choice.

Ann announced that she'd told Kevin that he had to apologize to *me* for having a temper tantrum. (That seemed very odd. During the day, I hadn't heard any sounds from their apartment... but noises have to be pretty disruptive for me to notice them at all.)

Kevin looked mutinous, squirmed, and dropped to the floor from Ann's arms.

Ann barked at Kevin, ordering him to apologize to me.

He just stared at me from where he'd landed on the floor.

After a few awkward moments, I said, "This is

unproductive," and stepped back into my apartment.

Ann shrugged and said, "Kevin, let's go home."

As they returned to their apartment, I wondered if I've been added to Ann's list of threats to scare Kevin.

According to our apartment manager, Ann had warned Kevin that the police would arrest him if he didn't start behaving better.

And then, *Ann called the police.* When they arrived, Ann asked them to talk to Kevin about his behavior.

That's so surreal. *What parent calls the police to discipline a toddler?*

Tuesday, June 26th

A representative from PSNH (electric company) knocked at Ann and Joe's door. Henry, the babysitter, answered. The representative spoke loudly. She said the power bill was overdue. On the 22nd, Ann's service had been scheduled for turnoff. That was days ago.

Henry said he was alone with Kevin and he couldn't do anything.

So, the PSNH rep turned off the electricity to Ann's apartment.

I called Maryann. She said that she didn't care as long as Ann and Joe paid their rent on time.

Last night, when Joe came home from work, I heard loud voices. Ann and Joe were arguing and I heard Kevin crying by himself in his bedroom.

I turned on the dishwasher so I didn't have to listen to a private argument. Then I shut myself in my home office, to work. We *must* get out of here. This is getting crazy.

Wednesday, June 27th

I'm not sure if Ann & Joe's power has been turned back on. In this record-breaking heat, I *hope* it's back on. However, their only air conditioner is in Ann's bedroom. So, I'm not sure that electricity — on or off — makes any difference to Kevin.

Today, Henry — Kevin's babysitter — was visiting Ann and Kevin. At mid-morning, Henry left the apartment. As he opened the apartment door, he said loudly, "I'll be back soon." It sounded as if he wanted everyone in the building to hear him.

Kevin immediately threw a tantrum. He begged Henry not to leave.

I looked through my front door security viewer. Kevin was clinging to Henry, wailing loudly. Henry gently removed Kevin's hands, stepped away, and started down the stairs.

Ann grabbed Kevin by one arm, yanked him back into the apartment, and closed the door.

I heard Ann's voice, but I couldn't hear what she said. Then, I heard three loud slaps.

I've heard thumps, thuds, and slams before, but nothing that was such a clear, crisp sound of slapping. This was clearly skin-on-skin.

It was over within seconds. After that, Kevin was completely quiet.

Henry returned within five minutes. I heard nothing unusual after that.

What's worrisome is how *little* this concerns me, now. It's as if I've become accustomed to Kevin being hit. I hate that.

Thursday, June 28th

This morning, Kevin was shouting in the hallway. His voice was so loud, my voice-recognition software picked it up, even though my apartment door was closed. I was working with my office door closed, as well.

I went to the living room to see what was going on, and opened my apartment door.

Kevin was leaning over the (third floor) balcony, shouting a word I didn't understand, over and over again. He heard my door open, and paused to stare at me. He said he was talking to the dog who lives in another part of the building.

Kevin was wearing underpants and nothing else. No one seemed to be supervising him. If he leaned just a little further over the railing, he'd fall.

I asked Kevin, loudly, if his mother knew he was outside. His apartment door was wide open. If Ann was in there, she would have heard me. (*That* was why I spoke loudly. I hoped to get her attention. However, it wouldn't be the first time she'd left Kevin alone in the apartment.)

Kevin shook his head and said, "No."

There was no sound from the apartment.

That's when I noticed Kevin's left eye. It was slightly swollen. It might have been a bug bite. He might have been taking a nap and slept on something that irritated his eye. He might have been rubbing that eye for some reason, and it caused swelling.

I could think of lots of *reasonable* explanations for the swelling. However, Kevin's eye seemed far more swollen than any injury I'd seen on him in the past.

Maryann had said that the police and DHHS couldn't do anything until they saw some physical evidence of abuse. Also, the police had asked me to call if I saw any further evidence of abuse.

I wasn't convinced this was *enough,* but it might give the officials the leverage they needed.

First, I called DHHS since they could get a

court order to protect Kevin. The caseworker thanked me and said to call the police immediately. They could respond faster.

So, I called the police station. The line was busy. After several more attempts to reach them by phone, I wrote down what I'd witnessed. I ran up the street to the police station and gave it to the woman at the front desk.

If the police investigated after that, they were *very* quiet. However, I'd resumed my work. I might have missed their visit.

After each incident like this, I'm feeling more frustrated and depressed. It sounds like Kevin is *more* at risk than he was six months ago, not *less*.

I've called the police. I've called DHHS. I've written reports, and then... nothing happened. Nothing that helped Kevin, anyway. Nightly abuse and daytime shouting, slaps, and thuds continue.

This diary helps reduce *my* stress, but a better solution is for someone to help *Kevin*.

Joe, Kevin's grandparents, the police, DHHS... nobody seems to do anything to protect Kevin. I'm just a neighbor. I'm not a relative, so my ability to help him is limited.

This is really frustrating.

Saturday, June 30th

As of this weekend, we now have *three* fans *and* a window air conditioner in our bedroom. So far, that's creating enough "white noise," so I'm not woken by noises from Kevin's apartment.

Or maybe things are quiet over there. That would be nice.

Meanwhile, the complex has a new, regular visitor. I've dubbed him "Handshake King" because he always greets his friends with a handshake. Then, a few minutes later, gives them another handshake before they part.

His skewed baseball cap, the saggy jeans, and his whole demeanor are so completely different from a man in a business suit, his congenial (but formal) handshake seems out of character.

Well, hey, maybe he's LDS (Mormon). In that church, people shake hands regularly. It's a normal, friendly greeting, especially in Utah.

We're far from Utah, and the way Handshake King smokes makes the LDS connection unlikely. I know I'm grasping at straws, but I'd *really* like a wholesome, normal explanation for this guy's behavior.

Handshake King doesn't seem to live here. I first saw him during one of Ann's frequent trips to meet friends in the parking lot. Each time she goes outside, she leaves Kevin in the apartment or on their balcony. A few minutes later, Kevin shouts for his mom. Ann's reply is always the same. She just shouts up at Kevin, "Yeah. That's enough, buddy."

Now, Handshake King has become Ann's main parking lot friend. In general, she seems much happier, too. I'm not sure what to think of that, but if she's a better mom to Kevin, that's a good thing.

Handshake King has been in our parking lot most days, especially in the afternoon and early evening. With me, he's always polite. He smiles and says hello (no handshake), so I'm not *concerned* about him.

But, he *is* a mystery. It's like Handshake King is the unofficial parking lot manager. I see lots of cars coming and going, and lots of handshakes through car windows. Doesn't he have a home of his own? I'm not complaining. It's just *odd*.

Monday, July 2nd

This morning, for about an hour, I heard the same things I've heard so many times during the past six months:

1. Loud thuds, pounding and thumping noises against the wall or floor.

2. Kevin crying loudly, protesting and then screaming, repeatedly.

3. Ann's voice, usually low and angry-sounding, with occasional shouts in a bitter tone of voice.

4. More thumps, thuds, shouting and crying.

5. Abrupt silence.

During that hour, the sounds moved from around Kevin's bedroom to the living room and then back again.

The thumps against the wall or floor sounded loud enough to hurt whoever was hitting the wall. It was a *sudden* thud, not the sharp, clipped sound of Kevin kicking the wall or bouncing a ball against it. The thuds were time-coincident with Kevin crying louder. They immediately followed Ann's low, angry shouts.

I feel that my calls and reports to the police and DHHS are doing *nothing at all*. However, I called the police anyway. Then I moved to another part of the apartment where the noises were somewhat muffled.

I *think* the police visited, but I'm not sure.

I hate this. After eight months, the situation is worse, not better. I hate that I'm giving up and trying *not* to hear what's going on.

In other news, the Handshake King hasn't been around for a couple of days. That's a relief. Generally, whatever he's doing is none of my business. Still, I'd like it if he's found somewhere *else* to spend his time.

On the other hand, when he's here, Ann seems happier and beats Kevin less.

Bleh. I'm weighing child abuse next door, against creepy people in cars, cruising through our parking lot. Neither is a good choice.

Later, that same day (July 2nd)

What a transformation! This afternoon, Ann, Joe and Kevin were on the lawn right outside their front door, laughing and playing with water guns and silly string. Even Joe — normally reticent and subdued — seemed boisterous.

Everyone was well dressed. Ann's hair was tidy and she wore makeup. Joe was wearing a clean, light-colored shirt, and he smiled a lot. Even Kevin was fully dressed in what looked like new clothes.

Except that I'd heard troubling things from their apartment, earlier in the day, I'd think they were a model family.

With a public display like that, no *wonder* some people don't take my reports seriously.

I'm increasingly convinced that it's pointless to try to get help for Kevin.

Tuesday, July 3rd

Around 11 PM last night, Kevin was kicking the wall. There were about 20 quick, even kicks in succession.

The first time I heard it, I thought the noise came from a car driving with a completely flat tire.

Then, about 10 or 15 minutes later, I heard it again and realized it was Kevin.

This went on, repeatedly, for about an hour.

If Kevin were on medication for his hyperactivity, he might be happier and get more rest. That's what one nurse in the building suggests. Maybe she's right.

However, I've decided this diary should include *normal* kid noises, too. I hear them most days, at least briefly.

Of course, I'd rather *not* be woken up by a kid kicking the wall, but — as a parent — I understand. Kids can be noisy, and it's not healthy to silence *every* sound they make. I don't usually write about those noises because they don't bother me. However, I'm mentioning them to balance this story and keep Kevin's plight in perspective. There *are* times when Kevin is a normal child.

In other news, Handshake King is back in the parking lot. Maybe he didn't go anywhere, and had simply stayed out of view. (I'm still not sure if he lives here now.)

I don't have a problem with *him*, just the friends who stop by to see him for five or ten minutes at a time. They kind of creep me out, if I go for a walk or leave my apartment to check the mailbox at the other end of our parking lot.

However, appearances can be deceptive. Maybe they're very nice people.

Either way, it's not an issue since — due to the extreme heat — everyone stays indoors most of the time. However, Handshake King's friends still make me uneasy, and he seems to be acquiring more and more friends each day.

Later that same day, July 3rd

Yesterday, the performance was the *happy, playful family.*

This morning, Ann kicked her PR efforts into high gear. Once again, she's well-groomed, wearing makeup and flattering clothes. Kevin is fully dressed, too.

Hand-in-hand, Ann and Kevin have been visiting some of the neighbors. A few people (with children) have visited Ann and Kevin in return. You'd think she and Kevin are the most popular people in town and they're holding an open house.

This afternoon, since Joe got home from work, it's more of the same.

Except that this is such a *sudden* change — remember, I heard sounds of violence *yesterday morning* — I'd think Ann had turned over a new leaf.

In my experience, short of a religious experience, people don't change *that* completely, *that* quickly.

Two months ago, Joe was throwing out a sofa and a neighbor asked, "Getting rid of that?"

Joe replied, "Yeah, and Ann is next."

The neighbor laughed and said something like, "A few people would pay good money to see that."

Joe responded, "It won't be long, now."

Then, about a month ago, Joe was in the hall, talking loudly to Henry. Ann wasn't at home, but Kevin was.

Joe described a conversation from earlier that morning. Joe said Ann had called him at work, shortly before he was expected home for lunch. According to Joe, Ann had said, "Before you get upset because I'm not at home..."

Then, Joe told Henry that Ann regularly leaves Kevin alone in the apartment. Joe said Ann gets text messages and then she takes off, alone. (Maryann had mentioned the same thing. She's seen Ann — alone, without Kevin — walking past the office during the day.)

Joe's conversation sounded too loud. It seemed fake. In general, Joe hasn't been very talkative. Now, I'm sure he wanted others to hear *everything* he said about Ann.

Was Joe being passive-aggressive? Did Joe feel powerless and want *others* to step in and fix his problems? I try to remember that Joe is just a kid, himself.

Then I remember *other* young parents I've known. I don't recall any of *them* having these difficulties. Usually, they learned to be effective, caring parents. There's a learning curve, but nothing like the problems I've seen with Ann.

However, other young parents often have a support system — family, church, or neighbors — to help them.

Joe's parents visited regularly when Ann and Joe had first moved in. Now, they're rarely here. Even when they are, their visits end with an argument in the hall and Joe's mom telling Joe that he needs to make some changes. Joe's dad goes out to his pickup truck without saying anything. Joe's mom usually storms down the stairs shouting, "You'd better think about what I said."

If Joe were my son, I'm sure I'd be frustrated, too.

Neither Ann or Joe seem to be very social. Not in a normal, neighborly way. Sure, Ann tries to act friendly when she needs something or she's trying to impress people. She's all smiles in the parking lot, talking with her friends through their car window, too.

Ann seems to have a few female friends, but they visit her, one by one. Sometimes, Ann entertains several men, usually two or three at a time. They leave before Joe is due home from work.

Joe only speaks when spoken to. He rarely responds when I say hello. In fact, he still looks at the ground, most of the time. Joe doesn't look *un*happy, but I've rarely seen signs of emotions. If he has friends, they aren't here very often.

So, Joe is a mystery. Most of the time, I'm certain that Ann is the sole abuser. However, I'd feel *far* better if Joe took an active role in protecting his son. Instead, he seems to be in "wait and see" mode.

That makes no sense. What would he be waiting *for?* Maryann mentioned Joe's anger management program. She said that could prevent Joe from getting full custody. Is that enough to keep Joe with Ann, knowing that his son may be abused, several times a week?

Today has been very odd. Something's going on.

Tonight, I feel like I'm watching their "happy, normal family" performance, and frankly, *they're good*. If I hadn't heard *awful* sounds coming from their apartment for the past eight months, even *I* might believe what I'm seeing.

But why this act? Why *now?*

One possibility comes to mind: I'm wondering if DHHS has advised Joe and Ann that this *isn't* a simple custody issue. *Both* of them could lose their son. Maybe Ann and Joe have closed ranks to keep Kevin out of a foster home.

Tonight, I'm feeling uneasy as the "happy family" performance continues. I'm trying to remind myself that, as long as Kevin isn't abused, I shouldn't care *what* goes on next door.

Wednesday, July 4th

Everything seemed to be fine again. My diary entry for that day was brief:

July 4th was blissfully quiet at our apartment complex. Both Ann and Joe were at home with Kevin. As usual, when Joe is at home *and* awake, Ann seems to keep her behavior in a normal range.

Thursday, July 5th

It's 3:30 PM. As I'm writing this, I'm listening to a manic, desperately unhappy child literally *bouncing off the walls*. He's shouting something like "Meh, meh! Meh, meh!" over and over again.

He's not fussy. Nobody's throwing Kevin against the wall. (Usually, that's a thud and a brief cry, followed by a sliding-down-the-wall sound. After that, I'll hear a whimper or — more often, lately — complete silence.)

Today, he's simply running through the apartment, throwing himself at the apartment door and at the walls, shouting.

Later:

Apparently, it's party time at our apartment complex. At least half the tenants are in the parking lot or milling about on the lawn. The sun is setting, and I see lots of people carrying beverages. Two boom boxes seem to be dueling, one from in front of our front door, and another from a neighbor's balcony. A couple of barbecues are lit on the other side of the parking lot, and I see a large, jovial woman — spilling out of her short shorts — holding a hot dog aloft on a fork. She seems to be offering food to the nearby crowd. Two very hefty teen aged girls are dancing rather lewdly with each other, and laughing loudly. I see a string of boys — about 8 to 12 years old — weaving in and out of the crowd, on scooters.

Everyone seems pretty happy.

Handshake King ("HK") is clearly the most popular guy out there. Earlier today, he'd shaken a *lot* of hands. Tonight, he's still making the rounds but it's lower-key. He seems to alternate between his car, an apartment where I *think* he's staying, and happy party-goers who act as if they haven't seen him in days.

Pippi, one of our other neighbors, is nearly as popular. On her balcony, the smoke is thick.

41

Usually, she uses heavily-scented vanilla candles to cover her smoking habits. Tonight, I think she gave up that pretense. Her balcony is crowded and everyone seems pretty darned happy.

Ann may be in the parking lot. Joe and Kevin may be out there, as well. With the fading light and the size of the crowd, it's difficult to tell.

It's nice to see the community gathered like this. In over three years, I've never seen so many neighbors looking this relaxed. I'm not sure if this was a planned party or something that sprang up spontaneously. Either way, it looks like fun. I may not *like* some of Handshake King's parking lot friends, but it seems as if HK deserves a lot of the credit for this party.

Even better, our bedrooms are on the other side of the buildings. So, the crowd can party as late and as loud as they want. My family and I won't hear a sound, once we climb into bed.

Friday, July 6th

Around 4 AM this morning, I went out to take photos of the sunrise. Handshake King was still in the parking lot. He looked a little worse for wear. As usual, he leaned against his car, texting someone. He smiled and said hello — no handshake — and immediately resumed his messaging.

I drove away, wondering if Handshake King *ever* sleeps.

Once I was on the road, Kevin's problems seemed far away. Sometimes NH and coastal Maine are among the most beautiful places on earth. This was one of those days. The air was still, and most roads were empty. It seemed as if the moment was frozen in time. I felt more relaxed than I'd been in weeks... maybe months.

42

I returned home around 6:15 AM and — as I climbed out of my car — I heard loud crashes from Kevin's apartment. The sliding door to their balcony was partially opened, but still... I was *at least* 200 feet away and the sounds made me jump. I doubt that anyone in the adjoining apartments slept through the noise.

I heard no crying or yelling. I'm betting it was Kevin, having another temper tantrum. Either that, or Ann was doing the same. In the past, she's thrown Joe's belongings at the front door, telling him to get out. It might be one of those days, getting an early start.

It was a little surreal to go from magnificent landscapes and absolute stillness, to crashing sounds from the neighbors... especially since it wasn't even time for breakfast.

Handshake King was nowhere to be seen. Maybe he went home, if he has one.

By mid-day, the noises next door had changed. Unable to work with the ruckus next door, I wrote the following.

It's 11:30 AM and Kevin is shouting, jumping off furniture, and throwing himself against the walls. Again.

I'd heard *different* crashing sounds in the living room about a half hour ago. I'm pretty sure I heard Ann storm out of the apartment after those noises.

Joe's car *is* in the parking lot. Apparently, he's home from work today. That's *odd* for two reasons:

1. Joe is rarely at home during this time of day. He comes home for lunch, but not at this hour.

2. Kevin is usually normal-to-quiet when Joe is at home. I might hear Kevin playing, but — when Joe is at home — Kevin usually sounds like a normal little boy.

This late-morning burst of shouts and crashes

is unusual, even for Kevin.

Right now, the dishes in my kitchen cabinets are rattling, and the chandelier in the dining room is shaking. I keep expecting to see cracks form on the walls we share with Kevin's apartment.

I'd call the office, but I'm not sure that anyone cares, even if Kevin might be damaging the apartment. During my *last* visit to the apartment office, Maryann and landlord *both* told me that, if the neighbors were noisy, I should call the police directly. They weren't very pleasant about it.

I liked it better when Maryann acted as an intermediary. I'm not sure what's changed. Maybe the landlord would be happier if we moved out and left him with tenants like Ann, Joe, and Kevin. I doubt that Ann complains about anything. However, since I regularly call the office about the noisy abuse next door, maybe I seem like a nuisance.

If we move out, the replacement tenants might ignore Kevin's noises. I'm sure that'd make life easier for Maryann and the landlord.

Meanwhile, I can hardly call the police because a neighbor's child is *playing*. The noise is annoying, but it's hardly *criminal*. In fact, there are no noise ordinances in our town.

So, I'm typing this as Kevin bounces off the walls and my china rattles in the kitchen.

Well, hey, my *good* china is in storage anyway. And, it's not abuse. I should count my blessings... right?

Seriously, I can't work with this noise. It's a good thing my book is ahead of schedule, so I can take the afternoon off.

Sunday, July 8th

Kevin's apartment seemed silent most of

Saturday. Then, at precisely 11:15 PM, I woke up with a jolt. I heard Kevin shouting in a panicky voice. Then I heard rapid thuds and thumps that suggest abuse.

They're different than Kevin's *deliberate* thuds and thumps. He kicks the wall. He throws things. Those sounds are rhythmic and even. I've wondered if Kevin's brain chemistry borders on autism.

On Saturday night, I heard the thuds that overlap, in rapid succession and *without* Kevin's signature rhythm. Those are the noises that worry me, especially when they're accompanied by Kevin shouting, pleading, and screaming.

Last night's episode seemed to last about 5 minutes — relatively short — but even 5 minutes can be an eternity to a child suffering abuse.

I hate this. I don't call the police because, even though they're less than a block away, I *know* they won't get here in time to hear anything. Last night, by the time I was awake enough to turn on the light and find the phone, the abuse was over.

Even when the police arrive in time to hear Ann screaming at Kevin, the police say there are still *no marks on Kevin* to document physical abuse.

How bad does this have to get before the police or DHHS do anything? And, how can anyone tell a normal cut or bruise from one caused by abuse? Ann can say that Kevin fell while playing. It happens.

I'm certain that Ann is verbally abusing Kevin. Usually, I can't hear what she's saying, but another neighbor does, and she's filed at least one police report.

According to Maryann, that neighbor heard Ann accusing Kevin of ruining her life. According to her, Ann shouts at Kevin, saying he's stupid, and so on. Like it's his fault she got pregnant in high school.

Supposedly, our laws protect parents from unjust accusations of abuse. I appreciate that. However, which laws actually protect children? *Where are the advocates for the child?*

Monday, July 9th

Last night, around 11:55 PM, 1:15 AM, and again about 3 AM, I was woken by thuds and thumps. Each time, I heard Kevin shouting and crying. Once, he cried "Daddy! Daddy! Daddy!", over and over again. It was heartbreaking.

One of the outbursts woke me up because the thuds and thumps shook my bed. Kevin is four years old now, but he's a strong child. I suppose he *could* have been hitting or kicking the wall that hard, but I doubt it.

During the 1:15 AM session, for the first time ever, I heard a clear, male voice in Kevin's bedroom. The thuds had stopped, but Kevin was still crying. All I heard was the male voice saying, "No!" One word. That's all, followed by a few seconds of total silence.

Then, I heard about five seconds of quiet sobbing. Finally, Kevin went back to *noisy* crying.

Two or three minutes later, the loud thumps and thuds resumed.

Each flurry of activity lasted five minutes or so, with long breaks in between. It was never enough for me to get up, go to the phone, and call the police. I don't call unless I'm sure they'll hear or find something when they arrive. Instead, I report the noises to Maryann in the morning. Whether she likes it or not, I want her to be aware of the continuing problems next door.

And, when I file reports with the police or

DHHS, I include my summaries. It's not a great compromise, but it works for me and the officials seem content with it.

Last night, the male voice sounded like a tenor. Maybe it was Joe. I've never heard him speak in a natural voice. Usually, he talks as close to a whisper as he can. That's kind of odd for a guy his size. Maybe he has to shout a lot at work and he's hoarse by the time he returns home.

Still, unless Joe takes sleeping pills or something, I have difficulty believing he's not *fully aware* of what's going on when Kevin is screaming and shouting.

In other news, Handshake King hasn't been around lately. I haven't seen his creepy friends, either. That's a relief. Maybe Handshake King figured he couldn't top the recent party in the parking lot. Perhaps he quit on a high note (no pun intended) and moved on to another location. Maybe the cops gave him an informal warning when I was taking sunrise photos.

As I was writing this, I heard loud, repeated door slamming from Kevin's apartment. Then, Henry took Kevin outside to play. The Henry-Kevin dynamic baffles me, but I'm glad Henry gets Kevin outdoors for exercise.

However, the door slamming has continued, even with Kevin outside. That means it's Ann or Joe. Children, raising children. *Someone* needs to be a parent.

Tuesday, July 10th

Last night was completely quiet. Either that, or I was so exhausted after Sunday night, I slept through any noises Kevin made.

Early this morning, Ann was outside, talking loudly on the phone. It sounded like a string of complaints. I'm pretty sure she wanted an audience as she spoke.

There was a time when I'd have listened, to see if I could help in any way. Now, I don't care *what* her problems are. I feel like an ogre for saying that, but nothing justifies her treatment of Kevin.

This afternoon, Handshake King is back and he seems to be Kevin's new best friend. Together, they're running up and down stairs, laughing, and then slamming doors.

Ann is using her happy, *nice* voice, something I didn't hear earlier

If Handshake King keeps Ann on her best behavior, even for a week or two, that will be a welcomed change.

Fingers crossed!

Wednesday, July 11th

It was another quiet night. In general, neighbors in this building have become increasingly happy, relaxed, and apparently blissed-out. It's more evident when Handshake King is around.

He *might* be responsible. The way he speaks to me — as opposed to how he speaks to other people in this complex (and those who drive up) — is still a sharp contrast. Lately, I've wondered if he's an undercover drug agent or something. *Something* seems to be exchanging hands, through the windows of the cars that pull into our parking lot.

He also makes regular trips to different apartments. I'm amused by how much better the women are dressing and grooming themselves, now. I'm equally surprised by how much time they spend outside, trying to catch the eye of Handshake King. My husband and I joke that our complex looks like a brothel. Lots of young women sitting on balconies, wearing too much makeup, tiny little shorts, and ridiculous high heels. Still, it's an improvement.

So much has changed since Handshake King set up shop in our parking lot, it's impossible *not* to speculate about drugs. Before he showed up, the neighbors were never this happy and relaxed. However, Handshake King is a mystery man.

In the parking lot, he slouches. His voice has an edge to it. His language is pretty coarse and he uses gestures I've seen only in hip-hop videos.

When he talks with me, his grammar is impeccable and his tone of voice is different. No hand gestures. He's *very* polite, even if he doesn't make much eye contact. He's a scanner, always looking around. I swear, it's like talking to someone's bodyguard.

Is it a stretch to think *that* might be why the cops, etc., aren't doing anything about Kevin's situation? Are they just biding their time, waiting for bigger fish to be caught here, before taking *any* other action?

Yes, I know how ridiculous that sounds: bigger fish or a drug cartel in this relatively quiet part of NH...? The couple with the flashy little sports car moved out *months* ago, and they were retired anyway. Everyone *else* around here looks pretty much working class.

Still, I keep trying to find a *logical* reason why my reports and others' don't result in safety for little Kevin. He might be a *badly-behaved* child, but *he's still a child*.

Thursday, July 12th

Kevin woke up and cried twice during the night: first, around 11:15 PM and then around 12:45 AM. The second time, Kevin was also kicking the wall.

(Remember: When I can hear Kevin crying, it *must* be loud. Every night, we use an a/c unit in our bedroom window, one box-style fan, one small turbo-style fan, and a tower fan. That combination should mask almost *any* normal noises from neighbors.)

Last night, it sounded like Kevin was just having a tantrum. The outbursts were brief (5 – 10 minutes) and I heard nothing to indicate that Ann or Joe were in the room.

As long as I'm not hearing abuse, it's pretty easy to fall back asleep.

Monday, July 16th

The blissful silence continues. Oh, it's not *completely* quiet but I'm not hearing abuse.

Last night, Kevin fussed a little. Then, around 9 PM, Handshake King knocked loudly on Ann's door. He kept knocking, off and on, for about 10 minutes. No one answered. Eventually, he left.

Today, Kevin slammed doors a few times. Other than that, everything's been quiet.

I attribute the relative silence to two things:

1. Ann seems very happy now. I hope it continues.

2. With our current extreme heat and humidity, it's *too hot* to do much except sit around.

Meanwhile, my husband and I discussed Handshake King's influence, and how much happier our neighbors are looking, despite the heat.

My husband commented that HK's appearance looks pretty contrived. The baseball cap is always turned *just so*. It's as if he uses a ruler to get the angle *exactly* right. There's nothing casual about it.

I replied, "I noticed that, too, and I've had my suspicions."

My husband, almost completing my sentence said, "And you think he's an undercover cop, right?"

I laughed. Apparently, my husband was thinking along those lines, even before it occurred to me.

We agreed that it's a long shot. This isn't New York City. It's *New Hampshire,* for heaven's sake.

Still, Handshake King's appearance doesn't make sense. Not when he's so different around me, and how his demeanor changes when he thinks no one's looking.

So, that mystery continues.

Tuesday, July 17th

After yesterday's heat, I guess I slept soundly.

All I know is: Last night, something made a loud *thud* against the wall in Kevin's room. It woke me from a *very* sound sleep. By the time I lifted my head enough to see our clock, it was 11:17 PM.

That's consistent with the usual time Ann returns from work and I hear abuse in Kevin's bedroom.

I remained awake for two or three minutes. I didn't hear anything else, and I went back to sleep.

This is one of those times when Ann's behavior seems compulsive. The longer the gaps between abuse incidents, the worse it is when Ann finally erupts. It's as if she saves it up.

Last night, maybe Ann *needed* to do something when she came home from work. So, she went into Kevin's room and threw something.

As long as it's not extended crying, screaming and shouting, and noises from Kevin getting beat up... well, I can live with this. Maybe.

I feel pretty sleazy saying that, but after nine months, I'm afraid I'm actually getting *used* to Ann. I'm accepting behavior I'd have reported to the cops just two or three months ago.

I don't like that. Not one bit.

Six months ago, there's *no way* I'd drift back to sleep just two or three minutes after hearing a loud noise in Kevin's bedroom.

Also, I haven't heard or seen Joe in *days*. He's probably there but quieter than usual. After all, *someone* has to be watching Kevin when Ann goes out... right?

Henry hasn't been around for several days, either. Maybe it's the heat. Kevin's apartment still has no a/c, except in Ann & Joe's bedroom. If Henry has a cooler place to be, he's not likely to hang out at Kevin's.

Henry's involvement with Ann, Joe, and Kevin... it's confusing. Henry is far too old to be a playmate for Kevin. And, even overlooking the family dynamic, Henry is too young to be one of Ann's lovers. He and Joe seem to get along, but something doesn't add up.

It's an issue that nags in the back of my mind. It shouldn't. It's none of my business, and this isn't healthy.

I'm not even sure why I remain so vigilant about Kevin's plight. I've given all *kinds* of evidence to Maryann, the police, and DHHS. I've spoken directly to Joe and to his mother. There's nothing else I can do.

I'm reduced to *hoping* Ann's moods improve.

This has taken dozens — possibly hundreds — of hours away from my work. I've had interrupted sleep since Ann, Joe, and Kevin moved in. And, my doctor says that my anxiety and stress levels are way up. This affects my focus, further reducing how much work I complete each day.

I *hate* moving. And, with my work on the brink of success, I'd rather *not* commit to a year-long lease at another apartment. If we're going to move, I'd like to live in another part of the state, or another part of this country. But, until my income improves, my husband needs his current job. That keeps us here, for a few more months, anyway.

It's a Catch-22 situation. I need more focus and energy to increase my income so we can move. But, unless we move away from the abuse, I'm distracted, and my work is faltering. So, we're stuck here.

Ick.

Wednesday, July 18th

I saw Handshake King at the grocery store last night. No hat. No exposed underwear, either. He looked considerably more mature. He recognized me, and we chatted about my career. Really. It was an intelligent, adult conversation.

The woman he was with at the store...? Either his wife or long-time partner. Clean-scrubbed, cheerful, and bright. She's *not* the woman I thought he'd moved in with, in our building.

I don't know *what's* going on, but it seems far more likely he's an undercover police officer or federal agent.

Last night, he was a nice, normal man, shopping with his wife. He could even be a dad, himself.

I'm very confused. If he's an undercover cop and Ann is involved, somehow, that *could* explain why the police aren't doing anything to help Kevin... yet. Yes, I've said that before. I think I'm repeating myself to feel better about Kevin's situation.

Of course, there's *no* excuse for allowing a child to remain in an abusive home.

Right now, the police aren't protecting Kevin. DHHS isn't protecting Kevin. Joe does nothing. His parents do nothing. Most of the time, Ann seems out of control. Lately, she's been a little better.

At this point, I think to myself, "Okay, when Kevin is older and goes to school, his teachers will recognize what's going on. Maybe *they* can do something." But, that's a couple of years from now. Will Kevin survive that long? And, if he does, will abuse seem *normal* to him, in a couple of years?

Thursday, July 19th

I spoke too soon. Ann has taken another turn for the worse.

The thuds — the overlapping kind, that Kevin probably couldn't make, on his own — woke me at about 11:30 last night.

They continued, off and on, for about 45 minutes. The thuds probably totaled 15 – 20 minutes of that, usually in 2 – 5 minute spurts.

No voices. None that I could hear, anyway. (In our bedroom, we still have three fans and the a/c running.)

When the abuse started last November, it was just Kevin's voice, screaming and shouting... along with the thuds, of course.

After that, Ann's voice became louder during each incident.

Then, I started calling the police. After two visits, including a follow-up from DHHS, Ann's voice became much lower. Sometimes, it seemed as if she was muttering.

Kevin's voice became more quiet, too. Then —

for awhile — he didn't say anything or even whimper during the thuds.

I'd hear him right before the thuds. Sometimes, he'd make a noise about 10 minutes after the thudding. During the thuds, he voiced no objections.

After the first few times I called the police, I'm pretty sure Ann saw them drive up and park across the street. She stopped the abuse before the police entered our building. There was nothing for the police to hear.

Last night, I had no good reason to call the police. The only sounds were thuds. If I were a new tenant, I'd assume the noises were someone lifting weights.

I wish I could assure myself that everything is okay, next door.

Over the past week or so, Ann has been relatively quiet. Kevin had a few outbursts, but they were normal for a four-year-old.

Joe has been completely silent. No greetings when he returned home from work. He says nothing. Ann says nothing. Kevin is silent. In recent weeks, that's become normal.

Not long ago, Kevin would happily shout "Daddy!" when his dad came home, and Joe would laugh, merrily. It sounded like the Cratchits' home in *A Christmas Carol*.

Now, there isn't a sound. That's why, last night and this morning, I had to confirm that Joe is even *there*. (He is.)

No conversations that I can hear. (The walls and floors are pretty thin. I can hear every nearby neighbor's music, TV, and usually a low drone when they're talking.) Either Ann and Joe and Kevin all whisper to each other, or they aren't talking at all.

Kevin has been oddly silent. Now, I don't hear

normal kid noises when he's playing... if he's playing at all.

He used to talk and shout at bath time, and play happily in the tub. Sometimes, I'd hear crying and a few thuds in the bathroom, before or after his bath. (About once a week, it sounded as if Ann was disciplining Kevin in connection with his baths.)

Then, Ann stopped giving Kevin his nightly bath. Maryann said so much water had been spilling out of Ann's tub, it leaked through the floor to the apartment below. Ann's floor and the neighbor's ceiling had to be repaired. After that, I guess Ann's solution was to stop bathing Kevin.

Then, around the time Handshake King arrived, Ann seemed happier and resumed Kevin's bath routine.

This week, the nightly baths have stopped again. Maybe Ann is at work, and Joe doesn't do baths.

They went from being the model family, about two weeks ago, to eerie silence. And, with nothing but thuds to report, there's nothing I can do.

I *want* to believe that things are better, not worse. The overlapping thuds last night were worrying. The idea that Kevin is resigned to the abuse, and not crying because he knows it makes Ann angrier... that's chilling.

I really hope I'm wrong.

Later in the day

It looks as if Handshake King has been in Kevin's apartment, at least since breakfast. Joe is due home, shortly.

Right now, Ann, Kevin, and Handshake King are on Ann's apartment balcony. Ann is using her nice, happy voice. Handshake King is wearing his hat again, and doing the "cool" slouch. They look as if they're a cute family enjoying the cooler weather and the sparkling sunshine.

As long as Ann is happy again, and the abuse stops... that's all I ask.

Well, no... that's not accurate. I don't *care* if Ann is happy or not, as long as she's not abusing Kevin.

Much later that same day

The building is rocking. Ann is slamming her apartment door, repeatedly.

It's the only sound I've heard from that apartment since Handshake King went... well, wherever he goes when he leaves here.

As usual, Handshake King left Ann's apartment late in the afternoon, shortly before Joe was due to return home from work.

Well, I thought that's why Handshake King left, today.

However, that's when the door slamming started. I looked out the security viewer in our door, and I saw Ann each time the door opened. Her expression looked angry, but not as enraged as I'd expected, given the noise she was making. It was more stern and deliberate.

I hope it stops, soon. It's so loud, my voice-recognition software picks up the sounds. In other words, I can't do much work now.

If the door slamming *has* to continue, I hope it helps Ann vent enough that she doesn't take it out on Kevin, later.

Friday, July 20th

Here's my latest theory about the silence next door:

I think Ann and Joe aren't talking to each other at all — giving each other the "silent treatment" — and Kevin is following their example.

There's evidence for this. Yesterday evening, Joe and Kevin went out for a walk. They left Ann at home. Joe and Kevin were completely silent as they walked through the corridor and down the stairs.

My window was open, and I could hear them when they were outside, too. Neither said a word — not that I could hear, anyway — until they were across the parking lot and ready to play catch in the field next door. Then, they acted as if the were just a couple of kids, joking with each other.

When they returned, Kevin was chatty as they climbed the stairs. However, about four feet from his apartment door, he went completely silent, mid-sentence. (Joe hadn't said anything since they entered the building.)

When Joe opened the apartment door, there was no greeting from anyone. Ann didn't say hello. Joe and Kevin didn't say, "We're home!"

And, for the rest of the evening, I didn't hear another sound from their apartment.

I think Joe isn't talking to Ann, and she's not talking to him... so Kevin isn't making any noise, either.

Later, July 20th

About an hour and a half ago, I'm pretty sure Ann left Kevin alone in the apartment. I heard her slam the door, go downstairs, and head across the parking lot towards the convenience store about two blocks away. (From a window in my home office, I can see as far as the crosswalk in front of the convenience store.)

Ann looked as if she was talking to herself.

About five minutes later, Kevin began making happy, normal sounds... like a four-year-old playing with his toys. It's the first *normal* sound I've heard from that apartment, in a long time.

Ann returned about 15 minutes ago. (Yes, that meant Kevin — a four-year-old — was alone for over an hour.) As usual, Ann slammed the door when she returned home. I heard no greetings on either side. Just silence.

Next, I heard Kevin crying and the usual overlapping thuds from his bedroom... the ones that sound as if Ann is hitting her son.

After that, everything was silent.

A few minutes ago, Kevin started jumping off furniture and throwing himself against the wall. (It's a different sound than when Ann throws him against the wall. Less impact, and no sliding-down-the-wall sound.)

I think Ann overheard the same conversation we did, a couple of nights ago. Maybe it just sank in, today. I don't know.

Handshake King (HK) was visiting another neighbor. He and the (female) neighbor were sitting on a balcony, not far from Ann's apartment. When Ann is at home, she's often on her balcony, smoking. Our apartment complex is in a rural setting, so it's easy to hear every word said, even several balconies away.

That night, the neighbor asked HK, loudly, perhaps for Ann's benefit, "So, what's going on with you and Ann?"

HK's reply was loud enough for everyone in our building to hear. "Nothing. We're just friends."

Then, HK changed the subject.

Today, HK has been somewhere else. His car isn't here. I think he's avoiding Ann.

But anyway, I think Ann heard that conversation. Now, she's upset. She and HK have spent a lot of time together over the past few weeks. It looked as if she thought it was a romance. It's *not* okay for her to walk out and leave Kevin on his own, or abuse him when she returned, but... well, I'm sympathetic if she feels betrayed by HK.

Sure, she's more-or-less married. She's living with the father of her son.

Still, Ann is a *kid*. She has a hard, ugly edge, but she also seems to be a lost soul. She has *no* sense of direction in life, and — apparently — *no* maternal instinct, herself. That's sad. I don't know where her parents are, or why she seems to be on her own. Maybe they gave up on her.

I don't know how someone like Ann gets help. She's pushed all of the neighbors away and seems to be living in silence with Joe.

Kevin is the real victim, but Ann and Joe seemed trapped in their own hells, as well.

Saturday, July 21st – early morning

Last night, everything was quiet. Thank heavens. I was worried that Ann was building up to an angry, explosive evening.

This morning, Kevin has been slamming the apartment door. I looked into the hall, and he was there, looking rather pleased with each slam of the door. His slams aren't as violent or as frequent as Ann's. I can (mostly) ignore it.

I haven't much hope that the noise will stop... not until Kevin gets tired of it.

This could take a while.

I've realized that this is how abuse continues. Unless the laws are changed — or the community gets more involved — interventions are nearly impossible. Neighbors such as Maryann and me can place calls and file reports, but the police and

DHHS can't do anything.

So, we live with it. It goes on and on, and we get used to it.

Unless something truly dramatic (and tragic) happens, it's just the "same ol' same old," day after day, week after week, and month after month. Even I am getting bored with talking about it.

I fight that, because accepting the "normalcy" of abuse makes me part of the problem.

I'll keep calling the police, and so on, but it's getting increasingly harder to make the effort.

July 21st – noon

I went out to check the mail. There was Ann on her balcony with Kevin, and Ann had a baby – about 6 to 8 months old — on her lap.

Ann lifted up the baby and shouted to another neighbor, "Look! I'm babysitting!"

Wow. Few things leave me speechless, but this does.

July 21st – later

Joe's parents showed up — a rarity, these days — exchanged a few words with Ann, and left. It didn't sound as if it was a happy conversation.

I haven't seen Joe since yesterday. Handshake King hasn't been around since the night before last, either.

Now, Ann is sitting on the lawn outside her apartment building with the baby she was holding earlier. Kevin is with Ann, and she seems to be watching a little girl around age 2 or 3, as well.

Ann is in full makeup, a tight tee-shirt, and jeans so snug, they're gasping for air. Her hair is braided beautifully. There's no way she did that herself.

Ann is talking loudly (clearly for the benefit of her neighbors), using her super-nice, super-happy voice, encouraging the little girl and Kevin to play together.

I may have to close the windows. I have no idea what's going on, but the performance is pretty disgusting.

Sunday, July 22nd

Sometimes, I'm not sure who lives in which apartments. So, until late yesterday, I didn't realize that people are moving out of the apartment where Handshake King was staying.

Funny, I didn't see him helping with the move.

The possibilities:

1. Handshake King *isn't* an undercover cop, and he's as flaky as he seemed, most of the time. He's vanished to avoid helping his friends move.

2. He *is* an undercover cop, and he's been moved to another location. Maybe everyone in his apartment is being transferred, as well. That's still my best guess.

3. He left for a few days, and the people he was staying with took advantage of this. They moved without telling him. (That idea amuses me the most.)

Meanwhile, Joe arrived yesterday evening, in a pickup truck I haven't seen before. He left with Kevin, and — if he returned — I didn't see him.

That truck isn't in the parking lot this morning, and I don't see Joe's usual car, either.

Next door, everything's silent. The chair Ann usually sits on is missing from the balcony, as well.

Is she still next door? Did she follow Handshake King to his new home? Or, did she just take off?

Maryann had talked about giving Ann & Joe a no-fault break of their lease, just to get them out. I had mixed feelings about that. Successive neighbors have been worse & worse, with each person who moves into that apartment. They seem fine when they move in. Weeks later, something happens. I guess they drop their guard and resume whatever's "normal" for them.

First, there was the young woman with regrettable taste in men. Every couple of nights, she'd bring a new one home. And, after a few days, her latest guy would be outside her door at midnight, pounding on her door and hollering that he needed to see her. Fortunately, she soon moved out. Apparently, she didn't tell anyone where she was going, even her parents. They showed up a few months later, looking for her, and they were amazed that she wasn't there.

Then there was the vacuuming fanatic. Oh, she was fun when she first arrived. She seemed very normal, with a coarse sense of humor but... well, fun. I liked her. Weeks later, she started placing signs all over her apartment door and the nearby wall, ordering people not to wear shoes into her apartment. Daily, and sometimes twice a day, she'd vacuum the hall, outside her door. If anyone brought any dirt into her apartment — or if she even *thought* they did — she'd escort them to the hall and curse a blue streak, accusing them of all *sorts* of things, including being "filthy pigs."

But then, she'd have loud, amorous encounters just inside her apartment, against the front door. Very loud. In a shrill voice. It was rather embarrassing. I think she brought in a roommate for a couple of months. The roommate seemed to normalize things for a week or so. Then, after a huge fight, both of them left and the apartment was empty again.

After her, the next neighbors were hard-drinking religious zealots. They were an older couple who dressed very dowdy, in shiny black polyester, and went to church every Sunday. They seemed nice and quiet for the first week or so. During the week, they'd go up and down nearby streets, knocking on doors and sharing Bible messages. The wife seemed annoyed when I said we were happy with our own church, but I couldn't pretend we were interested in her faith.

Things changed about a week or so later. They began to drink. Heavily.

After some very rough, loud, romantic interludes, the husband would pull on a tee-shirt with a vulgar message across his chest, and stand in the parking lot, trying to start his motorcycle. Over and over again, he'd kick the pedal just enough to blast us with noise... but the motorcycle hardly ever started. He'd do this for an hour at a time, driving the neighbors (and me) crazy.

When their lease was up, they moved. Kevin's family moved in a few weeks later.

So, I'm not looking forward to new neighbors, after Ann and Joe and Kevin move out. If they're worse yet, we'll move. Really, we should have given our notice last November, when the abuse started.

Meanwhile, I think Ann & Joe and Kevin should move back in with Joe's parents. At least Joe's parents could keep an eye on Kevin and prevent any abuse.

July 22nd, late afternoon

I guess Kevin *is* at home. Well, maybe.

For about five minutes, it sounded like Ann was throwing Joe's belongings against the front door of their apartment. She's done that regularly since she and Joe and Kevin moved in. We've become used to it.

It didn't sound as if Kevin was throwing toys or

even a ball at the door. It wasn't as loud as when *Kevin* is being thrown against the wall. It was just thud, crash, clunk, ka-thud, thud.... silence... thud, ka-thud... and so on.

That stopped after a few minutes, and I went back to what I was doing.

Then, Ann's door slammed *so* loudly, everything in our apartment shook. It felt like a small earthquake. Nobody left the apartment. It was just a door slam, louder than usual.

Next, Ann started shrieking at someone. It was her nasty voice and this time it had a real edge to it. She shouted, "No, you can't do that. You're not going anywhere."

Her apartment door opened and slammed shut again, quickly. No one came out.

Then, I heard thuds — skin-on-skin, as if people were hitting each other — and someone screamed long and loud. It was pretty shrill. It might have been Ann. It might have been Kevin or even Joe. I'm not sure.

My phone was in my hand and I was dialing the police when I heard someone on the stairs. I didn't *think* anyone had left Ann's apartment but I couldn't tell. So, I looked out a window. Nope, no one had left the building.

I went out to our balcony. I needed to see whether I should keep dialing or if it was just "drama as usual" between Ann and Joe.

A neighbor was in the parking lot, looking up at Ann's apartment. Another neighbor joined her, pointing at the balcony where Ann lives. Weirdly, that guy was laughing and — seeing me — he waved with a big grin. I don't think I've ever seen him before. I certainly didn't know him.

The noise stopped pretty quickly, and I saw Ann stroll out to her balcony for a cigarette. I put down the phone, but... wow. Until today, I haven't heard anything that loud here, ever.

I *still* don't know what was going on.

Tuesday, July 24th

Since last night (Monday), Joe's car has been in the parking lot.

Every time I look at his car, I'm astonished. I don't understand how a guy can drive past the police station, four times a day, every weekday, and *nobody gives him a ticket* for the missing rear view mirror. But, that's what Joe does.

It's not like the mirror issue is difficult to spot. From across the parking lot, the support for the mirror stands out in silhouette like a stick protruding from the car ceiling. It's clear that the mirror is missing.

There's *no way* I'd drive my car with that kind of safety issue, especially with a child in the car. But, as I've realized, my standards and Joe's aren't in the same ballpark. They aren't even passing acquaintances.

In addition, Handshake King's car returned last night, too, and it's *still* in the parking lot. Weird.

I didn't notice either car until this morning, so I don't know how late they arrived. It must have been after 8 or 9 PM.

Meanwhile, yesterday afternoon, Kevin spent several minutes lifting and dropping the toilet seat. He does that now and then. (A couple of months ago, it was a daily routine, week after week.) If he's *really* angry, he shouts and tries to rock the toilet off its base. Since the pipes are connected, *our* toilet rocks when Kevin shoves the toilet in *his* apartment.

Yesterday, I heard Ann yelling at Kevin — not in her ugly voice, just a stern one — and a scuffle involving the shower curtain. (The hangers screeched as they scraped across the metal shower curtain rod. I've heard it many times before. It's always like fingernails on a chalkboard.)

Then, silence for several hours.

Around 10 PM last night, Kevin was throwing things (shoes, soft toys, and small objects) against his bedroom wall. Nothing sounded like abuse, so I went back to sleep.

Except for whatever happened with the shower curtain, Ann was on her best behavior all day. Just a few days ago, all the leading men in Ann's life made a hasty departure. Maybe Ann has reconsidered her behavior.

Wednesday, July 25th

Yes, Handshake King is definitely back.

He's living in an empty basement apartment with no curtains. Everyone can see right in. He has a little furniture. We'll see if he's still here after the first of the month.

After Joe left for work this morning, Handshake King was at Ann's door in *minutes*.

I could hear his voice inside Ann's apartment, much of the day. (Joe didn't come home for lunch today.) HK's voice carries more than Ann's does. Today, he was using the same voice and language he usually uses in public. It's "street talk," not how he speaks to me. I wonder which voice is his real one. I'm pretty sure it's the one he uses with me, and how he talked at the grocery store.

As I'm writing this, I know Joe will return from work in about half an hour. That's why Handshake King just left Ann's apartment, so Joe won't know he's been there.

Besides, it's time for Handshake King's parking lot transactions. Business has resumed. As usual, he's more active in the late afternoon and evening.

I'm losing hope that Handshake King (HK) is an undercover cop. I think he's just a run-of-the-mill drug dealer. The voice, the clothes, and the mannerisms might not be real, but they're part of his marketing facade.

Now, HK seems unconcerned about concealing his transactions. Everything's out in the open. I don't like the signal this sends to HK's customers. Our apartment complex looks crime-friendly. After all, the police station *is* nearby, and the police drive past our parking lot regularly. I'm pretty sure one of our neighbors is a cop, as well.

In other words, the police can't *not* know what's going on in the parking lot, in broad daylight. I'm baffled by that.

I *want* to believe that HK is an undercover cop, and that explains all the weirdness going on here, but maybe this is just normal life in this town. Or, it's what our part of town has become. When we first moved into this complex, someone else was managing it. He seemed to move quiet people into our building, and the noisier people into the other end of the complex.

Now, we have neighbors such as HK and Ann and Joe. It's like the "bad neighborhood" moved in around us when we weren't paying attention.

Okay. Maybe I'm misreading everything. Maybe those aren't drug deals in the parking lot. Maybe I'm just too prudish about Ann's men, and the kind of language they use around Kevin.

And, maybe Joe knows what's going on between Ann and HK, and he's just glad that Ann stopped being such a shrew.

How did I get caught up in this soap opera? Rhetorical question. I've been looking for a good answer to Kevin's distress, and one thing led to another. That's embarrassing.

I'm *not* from this area. Maybe local standards are *really* different from mine. We have lots of neighbors, but I seem to be the only one alarmed by what's going on with Kevin.

Likewise, other apartments are *far* closer to the parking lot and HK's drug deals. If those tenants aren't calling the police, I'm staying out of it.

I need to narrow my focus to Kevin's plight, period and full stop.

Meanwhile, we haven't seen Henry much since Handshake King became a regular visitor at Kevin's apartment. I kind of miss Henry. He was a mystery. He used to look so starry-eyed at Ann. Then, he'd give me a silent glare, especially after I started calling the police about Kevin. Despite that adolescent behavior, Henry seemed to be a nice kid. I hope he's okay.

July 25th, late afternoon

Every time I think one of the people in this real-life soap opera has left the stage, he or she returns.

About 15 minutes ago, *Henry* knocked at Kevin's door. Joe answered. Henry walked in and announced loudly that he can't babysit tomorrow because he has a job interview.

Ann replied, "Awesome." It was such a monotone, I'm not sure if she was happy or being sarcastic.

Either way, it sounds like Kevin may be on his own tomorrow, yet again.

Well, he *might* be alone unless Ann asks Handshake King to babysit. *That* would be surreal.

Or, maybe Ann needed a babysitter so she and Handshake King could go somewhere. I'm not certain that she still has a job. I doubt it.

69

Thursday, July 26th

The apartment next door seems completely quiet. Early this morning, I heard Ann leave. I wasn't watching, so I don't know whom she left with, and whether Handshake King was involved.

Kevin might be at his grandparents' home or he could be alone.

That's the weird part. Ann portrays Kevin as a noisy child who needs to "settle down."

And, when Ann is around — and lately, even when Joe is — Kevin *is* an obnoxious, noisy kid. In fact, he's one of the most unruly children I've ever seen.

By contrast, when Kevin is *alone,* he may have a brief, manic episode. After that, he's usually very quiet. He makes normal playing noises. It's nothing like his running and shouting when Ann is there.

I'm baffled. Until now, I've never seen a child behave *worse* around his parents than when he's unsupervised. Not like this, anyway.

Today, I'm going to assume that Ann did the responsible thing and took Kevin to a sitter.

Friday, July 27th

Around 11 in the morning, Kevin was manic/hyperactive. Again.

Jumping off furniture.

Shouting.

Throwing himself against the walls and apartment door.

That four-year-old needs counseling, desperately. And, oh yes, I could use some *quiet* when I'm working.

Saturday, July 28th, early morning

The character of the beatings has changed. I'm not sure what that means.

Last night, it sounded like Kevin was being hit, repeatedly. Then he was thrown against the wall several times, more quickly and violently than usual, like a human rag doll.

The entire incident lasted less than two minutes. I heard one small shout and then a loud one. After the big thud-and-slide noise, everything was completely silent again.

It was intense and... different. I don't *think* it was Kevin having a temper tantrum. His noises are never that loud and rapid, even at their worst. I don't think this was Ann, either.

The alternatives aren't good.

July 28th, afternoon

Lots of changes. Two apartments will be empty. Both are in the same part of the building where Ann, Joe, and Kevin live.

Handshake King is moving out. For awhile, we thought he'd take over the lease in that apartment.

Meanwhile, one woman who lives downstairs — in the apartment under Ann, Joe, and Kevin — has moved out. It was a quick, efficient move. I don't think she owned very much, and what she did own... well, it was nicer than the average here.

She's suffered more than most of our neighbors. Apparently, she could hear the words Ann's said. The rest of us hear the thuds, shouts, and screams... but not much of what Ann or anyone else *says*.

I'm also sorry to see her leave. As far as I know, she was the only other tenant filing reports about the abuse.

So, with the apartment beneath Kevin's empty and Handshake King moving out, there will be new tenants, soon.

Sunday, July 29th

Tonight – well, technically it's this morning — at 3:39 AM, it sounded as if Kevin was being abused again. Maybe. I'm not sure. The noise definitely came from his bedroom.

In the past couple of days, the noises have changed a couple of times. It's confusing.

Similar to Friday night, tonight's thuds were loud, rapid, and intense-sounding.

However, the location has changed. Before, most of the noises were around the center of Kevin's bedroom, or near the door.

Now, they've moved further into his room. In fact, it's as if something is steadily pounding the wall, about three feet from our bed.

I was awake before the noises started, due to an intense skunk odor outside our window.

Then, I heard a series of fast, soft thuds coming from the interior corner of Kevin's bedroom. If I hadn't been woken by the skunk, I might have slept through those noises.

Next, Kevin shouted something like, "No. Daddy!"

After that, there was a single, loud thud against the wall at the corner of the room, followed by raspy breathing or wheezing.

Then I heard two or three loud, fast thuds. Kevin whimpered, but his voice sounded more distant, as if it came from *across* the room.

It was over in minutes.

I think someone *else* is involved in the abuse. The characteristics of the sounds have changed significantly. For lack of a better description, I have to say that the pounding sounds *male*.

My husband had been woken by the skunk smell, as well. We talked about what we'd heard in Kevin's room, and whether to call the police again. We decided against it. After all, what would the police find when they got here? Kevin would be in his bed. Even if Kevin said he'd been hit, Ann would say he was making it up.

And, I've been told that the authorities can't do anything unless:

1. Kevin has cuts or bruises that are clearly from abuse, not what you'd expect on a normal four-year-old boy who plays hard, and...

2. The police witness the *actual* abuse, or can get a complaint from someone who did. (That's not me or my husband. We hear the noises. Usually, the conclusions are obvious. However, that's not enough to meet the requirements of the law.)

Here's the problem: *Most* of the kids in this complex have cuts and bruises. They ride bikes and scooters. They have skateboards. They climb on railings and picnic tables. Then they jump off, or friends push them off. They shout and run and do all the things noisy, normal kids do.

Kevin, who lives a fairly isolated life, probably has similar cuts and bruises.

The first couple of times, the police arrived in time to hear Ann shouting and screaming at Kevin. She learned quickly. Now, Ann keeps her voice low — if I hear her at all — when Kevin is being abused.

There are no easy answers to the problems here. All I can do is listen to the sounds from Kevin's apartment, and write about them. I call DHHS now and then. Half the time, the person I call sounds concerned. But, even when I'm promised that DHHS will look into the situation and get help if Kevin is at risk... nothing changes.

That doesn't help Kevin. As near as I can tell, no one does. He's the victim. The neighbors and I are the only one who hear *his* voice in this. And, at this point, I think I'm the only one who's still calling the police and DHHS. Everyone else has given up, or they "don't want to get involved." They complain to me when I see them, but when I ask if they've called the police themselves, I'm met with uncomfortable silence.

I'd say "I don't know how they sleep at night," but — except for Joe — no one is sleeping through the noises in Kevin's apartment.

I'm just the only one actually *doing* anything about them.

Monday, July 30th

Last night, Kevin did something deeply troubling.

He behaved badly — in spurts — until someone came in and hit him. I think the abuse has reached the point where Kevin has become an enabling part of it. *Last night, it seemed like he deliberately triggered the abuse.* When Ann is yelling at — and possible abusing — Kevin, it seems like one of the *only* times her attention is fully focused on him.

Here's what happened last night.

Around midnight, I woke up when Kevin threw something plastic at the wall.

Usually, he throws sneakers and soft toys. The noise comes from the impact *on the wall*, not any damage to the toy. And, maybe I slept through those kinds of noises, last night. I was really tired.

The noise that *did* wake me was different. It crackled like a hard plastic toy hitting the wall. Kevin didn't have to throw it very hard.

Silence followed. I began to drift back to sleep.

Then, Kevin was out of his bed. It sounded like

he was running in circles in his room. Step-step-step-step, around and around, hitting the floor harder and harder with each circle.

That lasted about three minutes. Then, everything was silent again.

After about 10 minutes, Kevin began kicking the wall repeatedly. I think he was in bed, on his back, with his legs propped up on the wall. He kicked and kicked, rhythmically. (He does this so regularly, he must have *great* stomach muscles by now.)

That continued for about three to five minutes. Another 10 or 15 minute silence followed.

Finally, Kevin threw his toys again. Some hit the sliding doors of his closet. I could hear the clatter of doors rattling in their tracks.

(The wall between Kevin's bedroom and his parents' is buffered for sound by having the closets between them. The air space is about three feet deep in each closet.)

Kevin threw toys steadily, every two or three seconds, for several minutes, followed by a minute or so of silence. I'd guess that Kevin had to gather up everything he'd thrown.

Then, the toy-throwing began again.

Finally, I heard Kevin's bedroom door swing open and hit the wall, hard. That's one of Ann's signature actions when she's angry.

Next, I heard the usual overlapping slaps, punches and thudding sounds. It went on for about two minutes. Kevin whined, cried, and then shouted a few times. Mostly, it sounded like "No! Stop!" but his voice seemed muted.

As usual, this incident wound down quickly after one loud thud.

I heard Kevin's door slam shut, and he was completely quiet for about 20 minutes.

After that, he threw a few sneakers and soft

75

toys against the wall. It seemed like more of a gesture than anything with real intention behind it. The pace was slower than before, and the impacts weren't as loud.

Everything was quiet after that.

Last night, I have no doubt that he was acting-up to attract a response, and the response he expected was physical abuse.

The abuse must stop immediately and Kevin needs counseling. Otherwise, I'm worried that he'll make a permanent connection between abuse and the *only* attention he gets from his mother. The cycle will continue.

I've been reading reports and statistics about female abuse against males in New Hampshire. The descriptions sounded familiar: Throwing things, shoving, and hitting.

That's exactly what Ann does.

About once every two weeks, Ann throws things at a wall or door. Earlier this year, she joked to the apartment manager and to the police (I heard it) that she'd expected someone to call the cops sooner. She said she'd thrown all of Joe's belongings against the apartment door, one night. Ann laughed as she described it, as if her behavior was normal and funny.

I'm fairly certain that Ann shoves and hits Kevin. All of these fit the profile of a female abuser in NH.

Now, I wonder if Joe is also a victim of Ann's abuse, or vice versa.

As dismayed as I am by last night's events, I have a better understanding of what's going on. *In New Hampshire, this situation is not unusual.* Our neighbors don't report Kevin's plight because they know it's happening in lots of homes, every day. To them, it's practically normal.

This is chilling. For the last nine months, I've

watched the cycle begin with Kevin. Last night, it may have reached critical mass.

Tuesday, July 31st

Last night, Kevin was being boisterous. First, he was jumping off his bed, throwing himself against the wall, and running.

That's not unusual for Kevin.

First, at about 10 PM, Kevin didn't waste time throwing things. He went directly to kicking the wall. Kick-kick-kick-kick, steadily and evenly.

In a matter of minutes, I heard the "male-sounding" thuds around the inside corner of Kevin's bedroom. They were followed by a screech from Kevin, and then complete silence. I'm worried that these new thuds involve one of Ann's late-night visitors.

An hour later, Kevin threw a few toys at the wall and I heard the closet door rattling in its track. I didn't hear anything after that. I think Kevin woke up and decided to make a small statement by throwing things.

It's like a war is going on, next door, and I'm not sure how either side defines "victory."

Frankly, I feel *sick* that Kevin is probably doing things to trigger abuse. This outcome hadn't crossed my mind until Sunday night.

It's disgusting, but logical.

Wednesday, August 1st

Last night, I heard no sounds from Kevin or *anyone* in his apartment.

Early in the evening — before sunset, anyway — a waif-thin woman with vivid red hair left Kevin's apartment with a little boy. Joe's car was in the parking lot, but I didn't hear anyone say goodbye as the woman and boy left the apartment.

The woman opened the unlocked door to Joe's car and sat in it for about 10 minutes. She smoked a cigarette, sitting sideways on the driver's seat, with the car door open.

As she smoked, the little boy was running around the parking lot, pretty much unsupervised. He reminded me of Kevin, but his skin looked more olive and his long, curly hair was reddish, as well. Kevin is usually pale and he has short, straight, light brown hair.

The little boy ran aimlessly in the middle of the lot, where cars were coming and going. The woman didn't seem to care. I watched through my apartment window, deciding whether to call Maryann's office. Thankfully, cars drove slowly enough to avoid the little boy, but he seemed completely oblivious to the dangers.

He regularly stopped and tried to open doors of parked cars. All of them were locked. They didn't open, despite his tugging and the occasional punch to the door. Even when the boy was pounding on the car right *next* to Joe's, the woman ignored the boy. He picked up a chunk of driveway paving, and used it to hammer on a neighbor's car.

I started to dial the phone. Now, it wasn't just the boy's safety but a vandalism issue.

Then, the woman took Kevin's car seat out of Joe's car, strolled over to another car where a pale man with dark hair was waiting. He looked impatient. The redhead put Kevin's car seat in the back seat of the man's car, and the little boy climbed in after it.

A few minutes later, all three — the redhead, the little boy, and the man — drove away.

I'm not sure if the pair were Ann and Kevin. The build and ages looked right, but the hair color didn't match at *all*. (Ann changes her hair color and style frequently. Usually, it's a dramatic change. Her behavior, style of dress, and even her weight seem to change with it. However, *this* red would be far more radical than anything she's sported in the past.)

About an hour later, two *different* young men arrived — separately — at Kevin's apartment, about 20 minutes apart. Each of them knocked on the door, clearly expecting someone to answer.

No one did. There wasn't a sound from inside. (Joe's car was still in the parking lot, but maybe Joe was asleep.)

The second of the two young men punched the wall and then slammed his fist on the railing on the stairs. He seemed *really* annoyed.

One of them might have been Henry. I'm not sure. I wasn't paying much attention, really.

I try to stay out of sight (and away from my door) when Ann's male friends are visiting. Sometimes she lets them in, and sometimes she doesn't. Now and then, one knocks on my door. I answered the first time, but the conversation was a little worrisome. The young man leered at me, said things that made me uncomfortable, and I was pretty sure he'd been drinking. I shut him out in a hurry.

Since then, I haven't answered the door to Ann's men, except Joe.

If Ann and Kevin returned last night, I didn't hear them.

August 1st, later

I just returned from checking the afternoon mail. As I walked back, I looked up and saw Ann. She's smoking cigarettes on her balcony. She's dyed her hair red. So, *she's* the one I saw in the parking lot yesterday evening, and *Kevin* was the one trying to break into parked cars, and running around the driveway, unsupervised.

There was a time when that would have shocked me. Now, it's so consistent with Ann's parenting skills (or lack of them), it's practically ho-hum routine.

Ann's hair isn't *quite* carrot/Joker red, but it's a startling change from the peroxide blond color she wore while Handshake King was a regular visitor in her apartment. And, with the Aurora, Colorado movie theater shooting so fresh in everyone's memories, Ann's choice of hair color is chilling.

I don't think she chose that color by accident. It's another symptom of a young woman making poor choices to get attention.

Right now, Kevin is on the balcony with Ann. He's in his underpants, as usual. Yesterday, I didn't recognize *him* because his hair is a lot longer than the last time I saw him up close. It also has an orange-ish tint in the sunlight, not as vivid as Ann's new hair color, but reminiscent of it. I'm pretty sure she colored his hair. Today, he looks filthy. That explains what I thought was an olive cast to his skin, yesterday.

And, it looks as if Henry *was* one of the guys knocking on Ann's apartment door last night. He tried again this morning. Ann didn't answer the door, though I'm pretty sure she was at home.

When I went outside to run errands, Henry was standing just outside the building door. He jumped several inches, as if I'd startled him. As he walked away from the building, he kept glancing back at me nervously. Odd. Suspicious, I guess.

Today, the maintenance guys are renovating the apartment where Handshake King had been staying. I'm pretty sure he's moved, or set up shop elsewhere.

Unless I see HK somewhere else, I may never

discover if he's an undercover cop. It seemed less likely as time went on, but maybe he's a really *good* undercover cop.

And, as I'm closing this entry, either Ann or Kevin is slamming the apartment door, repeatedly. It's annoying, but part of a normal day.

It's kind of amusing (in a sad way) that I can't tell if it's the four-year-old or his mother.

(Really, if I didn't look for humor in this, I'd be even more frustrated.)

August 1st, late afternoon

Kevin is hammering on the walls. And, it sounds as if *he's using a real hammer.*

He's also running, shrieking, screaming, and shouting. I can hear him through my (closed) office door — *three rooms away* — even over the sound of my window air conditioner.

Ann keeps bellowing, "Stop hammering or you'll put a hole in the wall."

I want to shout back, "Ma'am, just take the hammer away from him." (To be fair, she's using one of her *nicer* voices today, but I think that's because the maintenance guys are in the building and can hear her.)

I'm worried that, feeling that she has to sound "nice" during the day, she's going to make up for it with extra meanness, tonight.

Fingers crossed, I'm hoping Kevin remains safe.

Thursday, August 2nd

Kevin was fussy last night, and I heard a few scuffles, but nothing dramatic

Today, some of the vertical blinds have been ripped out of the doorway between Ann's living room and the balcony. Ann is playing heavy metal music — from before she was born — just loudly enough for everyone in the hallway to hear it. Thankfully, with my office door closed and the a/c on, I don't *have* to be distracted by it.

Sunday, August 5th

For the past several nights, the pattern has been the same:

At some point between 11 PM and 3 AM, I'll hear a scuffle at the inside corner of Kevin's room.

I don't hear any voices or cries. I don't hear any slaps or punches. I just hear dedicated, repeated bumping or pounding at the interior corner of Kevin's bedroom. It lasts about 10 minutes or so. The rest of the night is silent. I have *no* idea what's going on. It's different from any of Kevin's previous noises, and different from Ann's abuse, too.

On Thursday, I visited the apartment office about a maintenance issue. I didn't talk about Kevin. I feel kind of sleazy, not mentioning the continuing problems. Next time I see Maryann, I will probably remind her that Kevin is still at risk.

If something really bad happens, I'm not sure if my silence is a liability. I mean, I don't want to be on the front page of the *National Enquirer* with a caption, "Neighbor heard violence, did nothing." (That wouldn't be *accurate,* and I know the facts would be somewhere around page 30, below some ad for migraine pills. Okay, I'm being sarcastic. Still, I'm keeping prospective liabilities in mind.)

Meanwhile, Henry is babysitting Kevin again. It's been over a week since we last saw Handshake King. That's still a mystery. After all, if he'd been conducting business here — and it certainly *looked* as if he was — wouldn't he return to continue business with his customers?

I'm not sure if that supports my theory that he's an undercover cop, or not.

Today, Ann needed a lift to work. Joe went out to the car first, and — to hear Kevin's screams inside the apartment, "Daddy! No!", over and over again — you'd think being alone with Ann was terrifying.

Two minutes later, Kevin raced out the front door. He stopped at the edge of the driveway, screaming. I couldn't understand a word he said. At least he was wearing trousers and a shirt. No shoes. No socks.

Joe, barefoot by his car (still no rear view mirror in it), stood there and stared at his son, expressionless. Joe glanced up at my window. I'm sure he saw that I'd pulled the curtain back.

Then, Joe opened the passenger-side doors of the car as if he were a chauffeur, waiting for Ann and Kevin. Kevin kept screaming. Joe looked disinterested.

Finally, Ann came out the front door and started down the stairs.

Kevin turned back and raced past her as if he were going back into the building. Then, he stopped about six feet from Ann.

Ann spoke with her *nice* disciplinary voice. "Kevin, you need to go to the car with me."

Kevin stopped crying and seemed to think about it.

Then, Ann shifted to her unpleasant voice, but kept it low. I couldn't hear the words.

Whatever she said, it was as if someone had struck Kevin. He began screaming, almost incoherently.

After about 45 seconds, Ann shrugged, turned her back on Kevin, and shouted cruelly, "Fine. Stay here."

Ann got into the car without a backward glance, and Joe closed her door for her.

Then, Joe crossed the driveway and ran up the front stairs. His face looked grim and determined.

When Kevin saw his dad coming, Kevin bolted, screaming in stark terror. He tried to run around the side of the building.

Joe grinned, scooped Kevin up, and threw him over his shoulder.

Kevin started shouting, hitting Joe on the back, squirming to get loose. Kevin seemed in genuine distress. In fact, I'd describe it as absolute *panic*.

Maybe it *was* playful, but it didn't look or sound like it.

Joe put Kevin in the car, fastened Kevin in his car seat, and the three of them drove away with Joe at the wheel.

I've never seen Kevin run from Joe before. Something has changed.

Monday, August 6th

Yesterday afternoon, shortly after Joe and Kevin returned, the sky opened up with a tropical downpour.

Joe said (loudly) that he wanted to go out to the car. Kevin screamed that he didn't have shoes and he didn't want to get wet. So, they didn't go out.

A few minutes later, Kevin started screaming and fake-crying that he wanted to go out and play in the rain. After about 10 minutes, he got tired and did something else.

At times like this, I can understand his parents' frustration... but not the abuse, of course. All of this is part of a larger problem in the home.

Kevin is only four years old. It's not too late to correct past mistakes.

When Ann returned home, later, there were a few door-slamming moments. After that, everything seemed quiet.

This morning, it's another door-slamming day, and it's barely 9 AM.

Tuesday, August 7th, early morning

I worked late last night.

Then, around 11 PM, I thought I heard a noise in the hall. I ignored it. At that hour of the night, I generally don't open my door.

At 11:20, there *was* a knock at my door. I looked out the security peephole in the door. Nothing was there.

Curiosity got the better of me.

I opened the door, and there was Kevin. He wore just a tee-shirt and underpants, and he was swinging a broom over his head. I'm pretty sure the broom had hit our door.

Kevin bolted back to his apartment, and I followed him. When I got there, the apartment was silent and all the lights were out. Not wanting to bother the neighbors, I said quietly, "Ann...?"

No answer.

Then, Kevin looked at me defiantly and closed the door, remaining inside his apartment.

I went back to my apartment and told my husband about it. He shrugged.

"That's been going on about twice a week. Kevin will be out in the hall, playing on the stairs, between around 11:30 and one in the morning. His door is open, the lights are always off, and I never see his parents. At least Kevin was dressed, tonight."

I stared at my husband. That level of child neglect is mind-boggling. Kevin lives on the third floor and the stairs — though covered with carpet

85

— are narrow and steep. A fall could be tragic.

In addition, there's no lock on our building's front door. (Someone usually leaves the front door propped open, anyway.) *Anyone* could drive up, enter the building, and find Kevin on the stairs, with no adults nearby. A nearly naked child...? That's a tragedy waiting to happen. We don't have a *lot* of registered sex offenders in our town, but there are enough, and I've seen one of them around our complex. Another one actually *lives* here.

My husband continued, "Sometimes, Kevin leans over the railing and shouts downstairs, 'Mom...?' but nobody answers. I'm pretty sure Ann goes out to meet someone and Kevin is on his own."

I mentioned that Joe's car was in the parking lot. My husband shrugged as if it didn't matter.

He had a point. Joe has claimed he doesn't hear Kevin's screams at night. So, there's *no way* Joe would wake up when Ann leaves, or when Kevin — unsupervised — is playing on the stairs.

We talked about calling the police, but what would we say? Kevin was back in his apartment, the lights were out, and everything seemed quiet.

I've made enough calls to the police and had nothing to show them when they got here. And, even though I've filed reports with the police, DHHS, and so on... well, nothing changes here, anyway.

I'm depressed and apathy is setting in. I hate this.

August 7th, mid-morning

I talked to Maryann, the apartment manager. She said she'll get in touch with Joe and his mother. She said she'll sit them down and have a talk.

We've been through this before, and I'm losing hope.

I've witnessed 10 months of abuse and neglect. I've learned not to hope for a *big* change... but a little one would be nice.

Right now, my *only* responsive resource is the apartment manager. I feel guilty, involving her. She's a sweet person, but this shouldn't be part of her job. She has enough *other* things to do, without setting up interventions about child abuse and neglect. And, I know her boss — the landlord — didn't want me to involve her.

Maryann said that *another* neighbor saw Kevin on the edge of his balcony at 11:30 at night. Kevin was climbing on the railing, unsupervised. (The drop to the sidewalk below would be at least 30 feet.)

That neighbor had talked with Kevin, and tried to get him to go indoors. He wouldn't leave the balcony. Kevin said that his mom had gone out to buy him some Lunchables. Kevin also said he didn't want to wake Joe because he'd be angry.

I explained to the apartment manager that Ann goes out at random hours of the evening, when she's not working. *Of course* she explains it as an errand for Kevin.

Ann is not likely run out to the store to get food for her son. Not in the middle of the night when only convenience stores are open, and none of those are nearby. She has no car.

Usually, when Ann is running out the door, she's texting frantically and some car swoops into the parking lot, picks her up, and they drive off together with the music blaring over the squeal of tires.

But hey, maybe these guys are her brothers. Or cousins. And they're being nice, picking her up and taking her to the store to get something for Kevin.

Gosh, even *I* don't believe that, but I have to say it anyway. I mean, it *could* be true.

I can't believe how cynical I am, at times. The frustration and lack of sleep have worn me down. This is not healthy.

Wednesday, August 8th

Big changes, overnight.

Late yesterday afternoon, I heard Joe's mom's voice. She was walking to her car and Kevin was with her. They left around the same time as Joe drove Ann to work, so I think Kevin was spending the night with his grandparents.

So, Maryann *did* call Joe's mom. That's a relief.

My husband was up late. At midnight, he saw Ann return home. She was accompanied by two men.

Around 2:30 AM, Joe left the building in his pajamas. He seemed to be carrying some work clothes.

Ann was on her balcony, shouting after Joe, "You're really doing this? *Really?* Yeah, that shows a lot of class."

Joe wasn't stomping out in anger, just walking normally. He didn't even glance back. He simply got into his car and drove away. No squealing tires.

I woke up about 30 minutes later. I heard loud thuds and crashes in Ann's apartment, but not in Kevin's room. At the time, I thought Ann might have been beating Kevin in another room of the apartment, or maybe even beating Joe. Then I remembered that Kevin was at his grandparents' home, and my husband told me that Joe had left, too.

The noise stopped, and I went back to sleep.

Ann was probably throwing things. She's done

that often enough.

I hope this situation resolves soon with Kevin in a safe, loving home.

August 8th, late morning

I called Child Protective Services, part of the Department of Health & Human Services, again.

I told them that Kevin had been out on the balcony, alone. I also told them he'd been on the stairs at night, unsupervised.

The intake clerk couldn't find my previous reports *or any file about Kevin,* in the computer system. Not even the file I was told about, the first time I'd called.

That's worrying. I'd assumed that DHHS was following-up to be sure this situation is resolved.

Did they close the case? And, when a case is closed, do they delete all related files? That's alarming. In fact, it's pretty unbelievable.

So, I described what's been going on, or at least what I've seen and heard..

The woman on the phone said she could file it as neglect, and a case of an unsupervised child. However, without an actual *witness* to the physical abuse, there's no case for that.

Well, the neighbors and I don't have x-ray vision to see through walls and floors, so there won't be any witnesses. Not unless Joe actually wakes up, one of these nights, and checks on what's going on in Kevin's room.

Yes, I'm being sarcastic. I'm also worn down. I've spent at least 100 hours on phone calls, reports and visits, trying to get help for Kevin, *and I'm not even related to that family.*

I wish none of this mattered. I wish we had normal, quiet neighbors so I could just sit here and work. Instead, I spent the past two hours talking to

DHHS and the apartment manager about a problem that's been going on *since last November.*

August 8th, early afternoon

Someone slammed Kevin's apartment door. A few minutes later, Henry stomped across the parking lot, swigging something from a can. He looked very angry.

I'm baffled. Is he angry because Kevin isn't there? For awhile, I've wondered if Henry has been visiting or babysitting to *protect* Kevin. However, if that's the case, he should be glad that Kevin is out of Ann's reach.

I feel as if I'm grasping at straws and reading far too much into events that are none of my business.

Kevin's safety is all that matters. Still, it's difficult not to get sucked into the daily soap opera, next door. It's as if I'm living in a real-life tabloid. There's always that temptation to see what's *really* behind the headlines.

Bleh.

August 8th, mid-afternoon

A few minutes ago, loud, banging noises came from Kevin's apartment.

Feeling as if I'm the nosiest neighbor, ever, I looked outside. Joe's car is in the parking lot, and one window is fully open. So, he's is planning to go back out again, later.

I want to believe that Joe is packing Kevin's things and his own. Leaving Ann — and taking Kevin with him — could be Joe's best option.

That would be such a relief. I'm afraid to hope that's what's going on, but it is a reasonable explanation.

August 8th, late afternoon

I should *not* have raised my hopes.

I heard voices outside, so I looked out the window, hoping to see Joe loading his car with his things and Kevin's.

Nope. It's Joe, Ann, and Kevin strolling across the parking lot. Joe is giving Ann a lift to work, just as if everything's normal. Ann is chatting with him, pointing at something across the street, pretending that last night's drama never happened. They're smiling. It's their "happy family" act again.

Now I'm *really* glad I called DHHS this morning. *Someone* needs to protect Kevin's interests.

For just a few hours, I thought Ann wasn't at home, and Joe was taking control of the situation and taking his son to safety.

I was wrong.

Thursday, August 9th

Late yesterday afternoon, when Ann had left for work and Joe and Kevin were still out, the *florist* showed up at Ann's door. No one answered the door, so the florist knocked on my door.

She was holding a lovely, large, potted orchid, in full bloom. I could see a gift card attached. She asked me what to do with the plant. I told her to leave it with the apartment manager.

An orchid plant...? Ann can barely take care of *herself*. Was that a gift from one of her nightly companions? Usually, they bolt out of Ann's apartment, pulling on their clothes, about 20 or 30 minutes after arriving. None of them look back, wave in Ann's direction, or even glance up at the building as they drive away.

So, an orchid from one of them seems unlikely.

If *Joe* sent her that plant, he has no idea how much care an orchid plant requires. Still, I bet it's his apology for walking out, the other night.

Ick.

Okay, Joe backed down from leaving Ann. *I get it.* But really... a gift like that? That's more than backing down. That's giving Ann a victory that Joe will regret.

I have no idea what Ann did to trigger Joe's departure two nights ago, but now she's confirmed that she holds all the cards. When Joe leaves, he'll always be back — sometimes with expensive, impractical gifts — within 24 hours.

Yes, I'm *irked,* and it's my own fault. For a few hours, I thought Kevin was safely out of Ann's reach. I thought I'd once again have peace and quiet to work (and sleep), undisturbed.

Then, around 2 AM, I heard Kevin running through his apartment. After about 15 or 20 minutes, his pace slowed. He probably went back to sleep.

No abuse noises. That was a refreshing change.

Today, everything has been quiet. Fingers crossed, it'll remain that way for at least a few days.

Friday, August 10th, early morning

Yes, it's around three in the morning. Yes, I'm awake.

I had a sinus headache for the second night in a row. I'm not sure if it's the new air freshener in the hallway, or the fragrance a neighbor uses to cover the smell of what she and her boyfriend are smoking.

My husband went out to the hallway and removed the batteries from the air freshener dispenser. In the morning, I'll talk with Maryann about it.

Anyway...

After taking a couple of aspirin, I decided to stay up until I felt better. That's when I heard voices, shouting. At first, I thought it might be Joe, though I've never heard his voice that loud.

My husband went out to our balcony. *He* thought the voices came from at least two apartments away, and he wanted to be sure everything was okay.

The female voice didn't sound like Ann. We didn't recognize the male voice, either. Those voices were *loud*. We stayed outside to figure out what was going on, in case we should call the police.

The woman screeched that she wasn't going to take it anymore. She ordered the guy to leave right away or she'd call the cops. The guy's reply was less distinct. Then, we heard a second male voice.

The word "Facebook" was mentioned, along with lots of cursing and lots of accusations by the female. She said she was going to hit the man if he didn't leave. Once again, she said he'd better get out of her apartment or she'd call the cops.

When she went out to the balcony and threw a shirt down to the sidewalk below, we saw that it was Ann. She was on her own balcony.

Kevin followed her, fussing that he didn't want anyone to leave.

All this, at about 2:10 in the morning.

This went on for another five or ten minutes. The language was astonishing. That kind of talk, in front of a child...? Wow. I'm still absolutely amazed, not just because of the language and the rage. It was *a voice we've never heard from Ann*. At this point, I think she has *four* different voices when she's inside the apartment.

Finally, the apartment door slammed. Then we heard loud footsteps on the stairs.

Two men emerged from the building: Henry, and Handshake King (HK).

We never expected that. Not in a million years.

Henry and HK half-shouted at each other, outside the building.

HK tried to calm Henry, and told him to go back inside and apologize.

Henry kept saying, "She had no right to bring my family into this. I'm just going to get my stuff and leave."

HK replied, "No, you need to apologize."

"I won't. She can't put her hands on me like that. It's not right. She's mental."

They continued to argue.

At one point, Henry mentioned something that Ann wanted in bed. He said it wasn't okay with him.

HK responded, "Yeah. I saw that."

Then he said, "Here, have a cigarette. It'll calm you down."

Henry replied, "No. I don't want to get hooked like my dad." I wondered what Henry thought was in that cigarette.

Around that time, Henry and HK noticed us and walked to the side of the building where they wouldn't be overheard. We went back into our apartment.

Less than five minutes later, Henry and Handshake King returned to Ann's apartment. She shouted (not as loud as before), "Yeah, well that's fine. That's fine." It wasn't a conciliatory tone, but it wasn't as ugly as it had been, either. It was the harsh voice she usually uses inside the apartment. So, apparently she'd calmed down.

After that, Ann's door slammed again, and someone ran down the stairs. I was too tired and annoyed to look outside..

In another hour or so, Joe will be up, getting ready for work. I wonder if he heard anything that happened last night.

My husband said Handshake King *has* been back here regularly, very late at night. He parks on a street in back of our building. That's why I haven't noticed HK's car in the parking lot.

Wow.

August 10th, late morning

This morning, I talked with Maryann about the problems next door. She shared some updates of her own.

Maryann thinks Henry is about 16 years old, but she's not sure. He's been homeless since his dad threw him out of their home, to make room for the new wife. She didn't like Henry and wanted him gone.

Joe let Henry move in. Henry has been babysitting, doing laundry, and generally acting as an unpaid servant for Ann. That's why I've heard less abuse recently.

Henry visits Maryann now and then. He'd told Maryann what he witnessed the night Joe walked out, earlier this week.

Here's the scene Henry described.

As usual, Ann brought a couple of guys home in the middle of the night. This time, Joe was awake and confronted Ann about it. Apparently, one of the guys told Joe that, since Ann was Joe's "woman," *Joe* should be the one taking her places after work.

That confirmed what I've been saying. Ann *has* been coming home from work and going back out again, leaving Kevin unsupervised. (It's *so* frustrating to tell people about Ann's antics, and feel as if they don't believe me. I *know* what I'm saying is appalling. It's also true.)

That night, Joe lost it and said he'd had enough. He gathered up a few of his belongings and prepared to leave.

Ann warned Joe that she'd hurt Kevin. Then she'd take Kevin somewhere that Joe couldn't find him.

Joe left anyway.

Henry remained in the apartment with Ann and Kevin.

So, now I know more about Henry.

Also, Maryann had another explanation for the thudding noises in the corner of Kevin's room, late at night. I think she got this information from Henry, but I'm not sure.

She said Ann probably takes her companions into Kevin's bedroom for an intimate encounter. Joe is less likely to hear anything there. (After all, if Joe doesn't hear Kevin *screaming for help*, Joe certainly won't notice some quiet thuds against the wall.)

While that's *disturbing,* it's better than some alternative explanations.

While Maryann and I were chatting, I asked if Handshake King might be an undercover cop.

Maryann agreed that he might be. Then, she remembered a fight between HK and another tenant. During the argument, HK called the tenant's wife the C word. So, if HK *is* undercover, he's *really* immersed himself in the role.

Maryann asked me to get the license plate number from HK's car, next time I see it. She's going to give that info to the police, so they can watch him.

I returned home and called DHHS to see what's going on with their investigation. The caseworker said they still don't have enough evidence of neglect or abuse. They've interviewed Ann and heard her side of the story. While they were in Ann's apartment, they looked for other evidence they could use, but found nothing.

They still need an eyewitness who's seen the abuse occur.

Yes, more ick. I'm beyond frustrated.

I asked what happened to my previous lengthy reports to DHHS earlier this year. The caseworker said she couldn't tell me anything else. It's a right-to-privacy issue.

For a few hours this week, I'd hoped that Kevin was safe with his grandparents, and Joe had started to move out and demand full custody.

Instead, Kevin came back, Joe returned as well, and Ann is still behaving badly.

How bad does this have to get before someone steps in to protect Kevin?

Joe and Ann – History

Taking a break from my current project, I decided to find out who Joe and Ann are... or used to be.

I learned that Joe was a *big* sports hero at his high school, less than 10 years ago. Google results show *page after page* of articles raving about Joe's ability to win football games for his team. Lots of photos of Joe looking like a sports star.

Joe *still* looks like a bulky, muscular guy who'd do well in sports. Well, except for the defeated slope to his shoulders, and how he shuffles when he walks.

That's kind of heartbreaking. I hope he can revive his dreams and realize them. It's not too late.

His more recent history isn't so great.

Joe *was* arrested for "simple assault" a little over a year ago. Did *that* result in the mandatory anger-management treatment that Maryann told me about? Simple assault..? Maybe it wasn't a first offense. Or, maybe there's more to the story.

Ann's history is different. Oh, she's been in the newspaper, but not for anything *good*. I found one newspaper article that mentioned her. In it, she was blaming Joe for the personal problems that brought her to the attention of the newspaper editor. It wasn't criminal — not *technically,* anyway — but it seemed pretty shabby.

Of course, Ann had a quick explanation and made it sound like it was all Joe's fault.

That seemed so ridiculous, the journalist didn't have to comment. It's the kind of thing you'd read in the paper, blink, and chuckle to yourself, "*That's* her excuse...? Wow."

But, it's clear that Ann has been blaming others for her problems for a *long* time. This isn't new behavior for her.

What surprised me was what I *didn't* find: Any birth announcement for Kevin. Weren't his parents (or grandparents) proud enough to post a notice in the paper? That's kind of sad. Maybe I overlooked the announcement when I was searching.

All I see are page after page of glowing stories about Joe's sports achievements, all the way up to his graduation from high school. Every one of them is pretty much the same. Joe was the guy who saved every game.

Of course, this makes the tragedy of Joe's choices even more real to me. He might have had a *very* different future. Maybe he still can.

Meanwhile, Ann is the one who hasn't changed. She's still blaming Joe for what's wrong in her life. And, she's brought Joe down with her.

I feel as if I understand these people far better, after this glimpse into their personal histories. I'm more sympathetic about Joe's dilemma, and less optimistic about the family's future. I'm not sure if it's good or bad that Joe never married Ann. Mostly, it looks like a relationship that should never have started.

Sunday, August 12th

Yesterday, Kevin left with his paternal grandparents.

Since then, it's been quiet. I haven't seen Ann or heard her voice. It's been a nice break. I'm completing projects, shipping them, and enjoying this.

A few young men visited Joe earlier today, or maybe they were there for Henry. They were boisterous and asked about Henry (loudly) while they were still in the hallway.

New neighbors are moving in. With them in the building, there are — once again — no empty units.

I'm enjoying the peace and quiet, and hope it lasts.

Monday, August 13th

Sometimes, I look over my entries and think I sound like the *worst* complainer. So, it's time to say something nice.

If Kevin *is* next door, I'm not hearing any sounds from him. I hope his grandparents took him with them on vacation or something. Though Kevin *is* a difficult child, he deserves a break from how Ann treats him. In fact, no child — no matter how unruly — deserves abuse *or* neglect. Kevin suffers from both.

With grandparents doting on him for a few days, he might even become a better-behaved child.

With that happy thought, I'm going to enjoy

how *normal* it is, right now. I can hear some of my neighbors, mostly the toddler downstairs and some children playing in the parking lot.

Those are normal noises. I don't expect absolute quiet. *No* apartment complex is problem-free or completely silent. Everything I hear right now... this is *normal*.

Normal is good. I'm going to savor this.

Tuesday, August 14th

Late yesterday afternoon, Henry left with a backpack and a plastic trash bag full of something, plus some loose items he kept dropping as he walked down the stairs.

A man with gray hair was waiting for him. Henry threw everything into the car, and the two of them stood there, talking. It didn't look like a happy conversation. After about an hour, they left. So, I think Henry has moved out.

He'd mentioned a specific bridge that he planned to live under. I hope he's not there, now. But, if DHHS calls me back about Henry, at least I can tell them where to look for him. (Of course, DHHS hasn't called me back in months. Not about *any* report. Not even when I call and leave my name and phone number with the caseworker's office.)

I have no idea when Kevin came home, but at about 1:30 this morning, I heard the slamming door and overlapping thuds that I associate with abuse. Before and since, it's been completely quiet in his bedroom. No voices, no showers, no toilet flushing, and no door slamming, except that once during the night.

What dismays me is how little I care, at this point. Frankly, I wonder if that's why DHHS doesn't do something, either. With all the cases they get, maybe they stop caring and just go through the motions, helping the worst cases *if* they can.

August 14th, later

Joe returned home a few minutes ago. Either he's taking a *really* late lunch, or he left work early. It's 2 PM and he gets out of work around 3 PM, I think.

The door slamming began almost as soon as I heard him close his apartment door. I have a lot of difficulty thinking that he's one of the door-slammers in that apartment.

I've personally seen Ann and Kevin slam the front door to the apartment, repeatedly. Both are childish enough to do that.

But Joe...? He doesn't seem the type. Maybe I'm wrong.

Today, the noise is okay. I'm taking time off between projects, anyway.

And, while writing this, the door slamming stopped. No voices, just silence. Again.

August 14th, night

I'm an early bird, not a night owl. My best writing time is early in the morning, so I generally go to bed around 8 PM.

Unfortunately, at least *one* person in Kevin's apartment thinks *now* is a good time to resume slamming doors. It's random. Silence for five minutes, and then three slams within the space of a minute. Silence follows for ten minutes, then a whopper of a door slam. And so on.

As soon as I start unwinding from my busy day and drifting off to sleep, I'm jolted awake. Adrenaline pumping, it takes me a minute to realize *it's just the neighbors.*

Then I turn over, adjust my pillow, and drift off to sleep again.

About five minutes later, the door slamming resumes.

I'm reminded of the title of that show, "Two and a Half Men," but this is like living in the same building with two and a half *children.* No adults are in attendance.

Wednesday, August 15th, morning

This morning, when I returned from running a few errands, I noticed a solitary mattress propped up on Ann & Joe's apartment balcony. I'm sure that's what Henry was sleeping on.

I didn't hear any sounds from Kevin when Henry moved out, yesterday. So, I didn't think much about it, until later.

Then, I'll bet Kevin had a massive anger session. I think he's the one who slammed doors and kicked or punched the wall for close to two hours, off and on, from around 8 PM to about 10 PM.

Even when it was going on, I didn't connect the dots. Mostly, I was annoyed because I needed sleep and the noise made sleep impossible.

Then again, *Ann* might have been the one slamming doors. Or maybe it was Ann part of the time, and Kevin the rest.

Maryann said that Ann had been using Henry as her personal servant. He was taking care of Kevin, cleaning the apartment, doing the laundry, taking out the trash, and so on. Maryann described Ann as a strict taskmaster, yelling abusively at Henry when he left a shirt on the floor.

(I've seen inside that apartment a few times.

The way Ann kept house, I don't think she'd notice if an entire *laundry basket* were dumped in a corner. So, Henry must have been keeping things *far* tidier than Ann usually does.)

It makes sense that losing a free servant would set off a temper tantrum on Ann's part.

This situation is so sad. There are no victories, just *better* outcomes among the possibilities. Despite that, people seem to choose the lesser options. All I can do is distance myself from emotional involvement as much as I can.

On this little sleep, after nearly a *year* of regularly interrupted sleep, it's a challenge.

Thursday, August 16th, morning

Last night, there were *no* sounds from Kevin's apartment.

In fact, Kevin's apartment has been completely silent since his meltdown on Tuesday night. No door slamming. No TV noises. No normal Kevin noises of any kind.

I saw Ann and Kevin leave yesterday afternoon, walking towards the convenience store. Both of them were well-dressed and Ann was holding Kevin's hand. That was a little odd. I don't think I've *ever* seen Ann holding Kevin's hand, except to half-drag him to wherever she wanted to go. When that happens, Kevin shouts and wriggles to get loose, but then gives up and lets her drag him.

I didn't see them come back, but I was busy. Usually I can tell when they're entering or leaving the apartment. They slam the door then, too. This time, maybe I was too immersed in my work to notice when they returned.

I'm a *little* concerned about what's going on, but I'm also grateful for the silence. It was one of the best night's sleep I've had since shortly after they moved in.

August 16th, evening

It's been totally silent at Kevin's. Not even a toilet flush.

Of course, they may make up for it later, but this is a little creepy. I'm almost certain they're in there. I've heard the occasional low voice, just enough to know the apartment isn't empty, but I'm not sure who it is. For all I know, it's Joe, all by himself. Or, maybe Ann left the TV on, and the volume is low; she's done that in the past.

I'm doing my best to keep working on my current projects. This past year has been filled with distractions. I'm far behind my deadlines for several project. I *must* catch up on my work.

For now, the silence is a blessing. I just wish I could exhale, with some assurance that Kevin is okay.

Friday, August 17th, evening

The mystery is solved, more or less. Either Ann took Kevin somewhere, overnight, or they'd all been giving each other the silent treatment.

I heard Kevin's voice in the hallway late this afternoon, and when Joe came home from work, it was "business as usual," at their apartment.

Ann was talking loudly, but — since I'm working in my office and there are several rooms between where I am and where she was shouting — I couldn't understand most of it. I *did* get the idea that Joe liked how nice the apartment looked when Henry was taking care of the housework, and Joe expected Ann to maintain things at that level.

Ann's not quite on board with that idea.

About half an hour ago, Ann's shouting turned

into a tirade. Then I heard her front door slam. I'm not sure if she went out or not. I'm working and trying to ignore Ann's bad behavior as much as I can.

Ordinarily, Ann would be at work at this hour. Either she has a few days off or she lost her job again.

Meanwhile, Kevin is in the bathtub, kicking the wall or throwing very solid objects at it. I didn't hear any bathwater running, so I'm pretty sure Kevin is standing in the tub, wearing shoes. I bet he likes kicking the wall in there because even the smallest sound echoes.

He's a quirky kid. Despite his bad behavior, I like him.

I hope someone starts teaching Kevin soccer moves. With all the kicking Kevin does, he'd be a natural at it.

August 17th, later

Two people in business attire, with clipboards and files in hand, were knocking at Ann's door. There was no answer.

Then, the visitors knocked at other doors in the building, including my door. Apparently, I was the first one to answer, and they asked if Ann lived in that apartment, and if Kevin did, too.

I'm guessing it was DHHS, Child Protective Services. I hope so, and — even more — *I hope they return.*

I'm afraid of getting my hopes up, but *anything* like this is encouraging.

Kevin deserves better treatment than he's received from Ann.

Saturday, August 18th

If Ann and Kevin returned yesterday, I didn't hear them.

Joe didn't come home for lunch. I didn't hear him return from work at the end of the day. He hadn't returned by the time I went to bed last night, either.

This morning, his car is in the parking lot but no sounds can be heard from his apartment.

Something's changed, and I'm not sure what, yet.

Sunday, August 19th, morning

As of 9:30 *last* night (Saturday), Joe's car was still in the parking lot, but I heard no sounds next door. On the front side of the apartment, all of the lights were off and I saw no flickering lights from their TV. (I'm *not* nosy enough to walk around to the back of the building to see if the bedroom lights were on.)

As of 9 AM this morning, it's still eerily quiet. By now, I'd usually hear the shower or at least the toilet flushing.

Either Kevin (and perhaps Ann) aren't there, or they're in "silent treatment" mode again.

I'm going to enjoy this while it lasts, but it's still kind of creepy.

August 19th, late afternoon

Yes, something is definitely going on. Ann and Kevin returned a few minutes ago.

Her behavior and routines are very different. I hope she's not setting things up so she can vanish with Kevin and leave no trail. From what Maryann said, Ann has been threatening Joe with that.

Apparently, Ann's been griping that her neighbors are watching her, too. She says she's going to move when the lease is up, so no one will call the cops on her.

Please. If she conducted herself more responsibly, we'd *all* be happy to remove the police from speed-dial. I'm sure they'd like being spared the *apparently* pointless treks up our apartment stairs, as well.

This has become frustrating for everyone involved. Ann can't seem to stop. Kevin can't stop her, either. The police don't have the authority to do anything, unless there's overwhelming evidence that a child is being abused, *right at that moment*. Joe and his parents don't seem to protect Kevin. And, none of my calls and reports seem to help anyone at all.

Wednesday, August 22nd, morning

The strange silence continues.

That could be *really* good news. I've heard no abuse at Kevin's apartment since they acquired new neighbors downstairs. Maybe it's a coincidence, or maybe Ann decided to turn over a new leaf since only two neighbors (in our entire building) — including me — remain from the group who'd been reporting Ann to the police, DHHS, Joe's mother, or the apartment manager.

Ann isn't stupid. She know this could be a fresh start for her. She has a chance to clean up her act and make it seem as if she's *not* a bad parent, and the rest of us were just picking on her.

That's fine with me. I'll be *delighted* if she's turned over a new leaf. Everyone deserves a second chance.

Meanwhile, it seems as if *something else* is changing in Kevin's family. I don't know if they're moving, splitting up, or what. Their lease is up at the start of October. I hope they're moving.

For now, no one seems to be in the apartment, much of the time.

Ann and Kevin were somewhere else on Monday morning. They came home shortly before Joe returned from work. Then, all three went out when it was time for Ann to go to work (I think), but no one came home while I was awake. I went to bed at 9:30 PM, so I have no idea when Joe — or anyone else in that apartment — returned.

Around 3 in the morning (very early on Tuesday), I heard a child running around in a nearby apartment. I'm guessing that it was Kevin, but I don't know. I heard nothing else until Joe got up, around 4:30 AM.

Today, there are no sounds of abuse... that's a good thing. We'll see what happens. For now, I don't have much to report because it sounds as if Ann and Kevin are rarely at home. Henry hasn't been back, and I'm pretty sure Handshake King hasn't returned since the big middle-of-the-night fight involving Henry, on August 10th.

August 22nd, mid-morning

Ann and Kevin just left. It looked like Ann was going to work, but she was getting a lift with an on-again, off-again female friend. Maybe Ann was called in, early. Or, maybe this is more of whatever's going on now.

Ann's backpack seemed surprisingly full and heavy today. As she walked, she leaned far forward to offset the pull of the backpack. She might be moving some of her belongings out of the apartment, a little at a time. Today, that's how it looks.

The interesting thing is how *carefully* Ann makes sure Kevin is secure in his car seat, when someone *other* than Joe is watching. If it's just

Ann, or Ann and Joe plus Kevin, Ann seems uninterested. Maybe Kevin gets into his car seat himself; maybe he doesn't. Generally, it seems as if Ann has no emotional attachment to her child.

Thursday, August 23rd, evening

Around 7:45 PM, Ann returned home with Kevin.

When she opened the door to the apartment, the living room was completely dark. Kevin asked why. Ann replied with a sneer, "Looks like Dad didn't pay *his* bill. *Again.*"

About 30 minutes later, two women visited Ann and Kevin. I think Joe's father was at the wheel of the pickup truck they arrived in, but I'm not sure. It was very noisy in the hallway, so I looked out the security viewer. Two women, no men.

When Ann's door opened, I could see light in the hallway. Apparently, Ann had rushed to judgment. Again. The speed with which she blames Joe — loudly — for *everything...* it's astonishing. As if the electric bill has nothing to do with her. It's *his* bill and *his* fault, just as she blamed him for the missing can opener, several weeks ago, and — back when Ann was in the newspaper, she blamed Joe for *that* situation, as well. For Ann, it's become a reflex.

Meanwhile, unless Joe parked his car in *another* part of the lot, he didn't come home from work tonight.

I'm still not sure what's going on, but everything that was routine for 8+ months has changed. That's okay. The only really important change is that *Kevin isn't being abused.*

I want to exhale and say, "Finally, they've become responsible parents." I'm not ready to do that because I've been fooled by Ann's act, in the past. I *want* to believe the best of people, especially a mom, but Ann has proved to me that some women either don't have the maternal instinct, or they can't let it rise above the tyranny of their acting-out.

I can't let this become my problem. I've fretted over this, filed several police reports and placed lots of calls to DHHS. I've described the problem to Joe, his mother, Maryann, and our landlord.

Between that and the interrupted sleep, I'm feeling stressed, exhausted, frustrated, and verging on apathy.

Whether we move or they move, I'm tired of this. I have to remember that Kevin's not in peril... nothing *life-threatening,* anyway. And, for whatever reason, we neighbors seem to care more about Kevin's well-being than his parents, grandparents, the police, or DHHS do.

I'm going to bed now, and expect that it will be another quiet night.

Friday, August 24th

The good new is: Kevin was acting-up some, last night, and I heard no follow-up abuse.

Around 10:15 last night, someone was either crawling or groping his (or her) way up the stairs. The thuds on the stairs were pretty solid and the breathing sounded labored. I could hear the sound of fabric pressed against the wall, and dragging along.

I'm pretty sure it was Joe, coming home drunk. It's crossed my mind that Joe may be a drinker. That would explain why he sleeps soundly, even when his son screams for help. Maybe Joe passes out each night and *nothing* would wake him.

I'd like to think better of Joe, but I have little or nothing to work with. He wasn't at *all* surprised when I first told him about Ann's abuse, but he also claimed he'd never heard it. That just *doesn't make sense.*

But anyway, around 11:15 PM, I heard Kevin running around the apartment. It lasted about five minutes and then everything was quiet. About 10 minutes later, I heard what sounded like a ball being bounced against a wall in their apartment. Maybe Kevin was kicking (or hitting) the wall with a sneaker that had a very spongy sole. The sound was slightly hollow and sproing-y.

It wasn't very loud, so I drifted back to sleep.

I heard nothing else after that. That's encouraging.

August 24th, afternoon

Joe left about five minutes ago. I'm assuming he's on his way to work. Either he's been moved to a later shift — unlikely to start at this hour of the day — or he's just now getting up. He stumbled once on his way to his car, but otherwise seemed happy enough, swinging the lanyard attached to his keys.

Everything looks normal.

No door slams. If anyone was in the apartment when Joe left, I didn't hear them. No one said goodbye to Joe, and he said nothing as he exited his apartment. He didn't look up at his apartment balcony to see if Kevin was waving goodbye, either.

I suppose that's nothing unusual, except the hour. I was on the patio, taking a break. Otherwise, I wouldn't have noticed him at all.

August 24th, later

Ann returned with Kevin, about 20 minutes after Joe left. *Lots* of door slamming was involved.

After that, there was total silence. Not even the toilet flushing or a faucet or shower running. Very odd.

Sometimes, I feel as if I'm living in a foreign movie with no subtitles.

Right now, I'm trying to wrap my brain around the idea that *maybe Kevin's plight isn't so unusual* here. The way our apartment is placed, we just *happen* to hear what's going on in Kevin's apartment. For all we know, crazier things are going on in other apartments, but we just don't hear them.

Or not. Maybe we are the only ones who hear Ann and Kevin, and everyone else leads a quiet, normal life, oblivious to what's going on with their neighbors.

Then again, maybe they take "good fences make good neighbors" to an extreme that seems odd to *us*... and my husband and I are the ones who look odd to *them*.

Lack of sleep is definitely catching up with me. Well, that and the fact that I've been the *only* one calling the police recently, reporting sounds of abuse in Kevin's apartment. I don't like that.

I live in a small, quiet town because *I like my privacy.* I don't *want* to be the subject of attention. But, with each call, I feel as if I stand out more and more, among neighbors who either don't hear what's going on with Kevin, or don't care. And, the police are frustrated because *they* can't do anything, either.

Monday, August 27th

I thought things were going to be quiet, but I was disappointed. I heard two scuffles in Kevin's room last night. (That was Sunday night, August 26th.)

One was at 1 AM, and the other was around 2:30 AM. Both included overlapping thuds that, in the past, sounded like physical abuse.

When I was woken at 2:30 AM, I heard Kevin's anguished (and very loud) shout, "Mommy!" That was followed by four or five thuds like the anger was quickly winding down. The rest of the night seemed silent.

Maybe it wasn't abuse. I'm not sure.

My biggest fear is that Kevin is being abused by some of the men Ann brings home. Sometimes the character of the noises changes significantly, but it still sounds like abuse.

See, this had been a public, online diary for others to read. I thought it might get the attention of DHHS or someone who could help Kevin.

Then, I started checking which websites were linking to my blog.

The majority were porn sites. Some of the homepages included images of young adults... *really* young adults, and some featured S&M. That's when — with horror — I realized that some people might be titillated, reading about Kevin's abuse.

(Right away, I removed my blog from public view.)

I really hope I'm wrong, and *awfulizing* because I was so shocked when I saw where my traffic was coming from.

Perhaps it's just my lack of sleep talking. I hope so.

A year ago, nothing like this would have

crossed my mind... not about anyone.

I hate what's going on next door, and I hate how it's affected me.

I hate searching for what I can do about Kevin's plight, within the law, and the answer is: Not much. Not without help from *someone* in Kevin's family.

The whole thing makes me want to throw up. This is *far* removed from the world that I grew up in, but — now that I know this goes on — I can't *not* do something about it. I want to bring this to the attention of people who can change the laws so New Hampshire's children are protected from abuse.

Right now, they're not. Not well *enough*, anyway.

But mostly, I can't ignore Kevin's pleas for help.

August 27th, evening

I think Kevin's apartment is generally empty, at least during the day.

Despite record-breaking heat and humidity, and no a/c except in Ann & Joe's bedroom, the sliding glass door — the only source of fresh air in the front of the apartment — is always closed. So, I'm hoping that Ann and Kevin aren't at home.

Joe is still there, at least to sleep. He left for work as usual, early this morning.

My husband thinks he saw Ann dropped off in the parking lot, *really* late last night. She went out with her characteristic door slam, around nine this morning.

I have no idea where Kevin is, and — if he's in the apartment — if he has a babysitter during the day.

Tension is in the air. Sometimes, it practically

crackles.

Whatever changed a couple of weeks ago, it's still going on. This has a very final feeling to it.

Thursday, August 30th, mid-morning

For the past two nights, Ann, Joe and Kevin have looked like a very normal family as they return home each evening.

Maybe Ann has a day job now, and Kevin is in daycare? I don't know.

They walk up the stairs, talking in normal voices about normal things. Joe chats with Kevin about Kevin's day. Kevin asks Joe a few questions. Ann isn't pushing her way into the conversation.

Two nights ago, Ann said something about carrying the box (boxes?) carefully.

Last night, Kevin asked his dad something about "in the new house." Joe replied, and mentioned something about keys.

I was watching TV, so I only heard what was said when they were directly *at* their front door, where sound seems to echo into my apartment. And, I wasn't listening closely, so I could be completely wrong about the context.

For all I know, they're talking about a friend or relative who has a new house. Or, this might confirm my suspicions (and Maryann's) that they're moving.

Late last night — around 2 in the morning, I think — there was another scuffle in Kevin's room. It's loud enough to wake me, but not clear enough to say that it's *abuse*. No voices, just several rapid thuds, slightly overlapping, in the corner of the room. They're not the same kind of rhythmic as when Kevin is kicking the wall. Other than that, I haven't a clue what's going on.

It's a brief outburst each time, lasting less than a minute or two after I've been woken up. And, it's over so quickly, I don't bother to roll over, lift my head, and look at the clock across the room.

I want to believe that the abuse has stopped, but — given what I've heard regularly for most of the past year — I doubt it.

August 30th, afternoon

I was sitting on the sofa, eating a late lunch, when Ann slammed the door (loudly) and clomped down the stairs. Then, she shuffled her way out to Joe's car, dragging her black flip-flops with each step. She was in her usual long-sleeved, black hoodie outfit, over what looks like a dark pink blouse. The hood was up, almost fully concealing her face, reminiscent of the Emperor in *Star Wars*.

It's at least 80 degrees out.

Ann's hunched-over gait seemed like a grand performance as she half-stumbled to Joe's car, across the parking lot. The body language didn't look right.

Even with the hood down, it was easy to see that she was glancing around, looking for an audience. There wasn't any.

Then, Ann leaned on the hood of Joe's car with her back to the building, kind of doubled up.

Finally a tall, muscular high school kid walked near our driveway. Ann exaggerated her pose, clearly looking for sympathy or an offer of help.

The high school kid glanced at her and nervously rubbed his hand over his short blond hair. Then he turned his head, deliberately looking across the street until he was well on the other side of where Ann stood.

Ann straightened up for a second, looking after

116

him. When he reached the corner of the building where he couldn't see Ann, her face crumpled. I think it was a wake-up call for her. At that moment, she probably realized she wasn't attractive to high schoolers anymore.

I felt sorry for her.

Ann returned to her hunched-over pose for a few more minutes, but no one else came along. She opened the passenger side door, and stood there, looking around. The parking lot was empty, except for the cable guy coming and going, and he didn't seem interested in what Ann was doing.

Finally, Ann sat in Joe's car until she heard Joe and Kevin coming out of the building. (It's easy to tell when Kevin comes & goes. He slams the door so enthusiastically, it can be heard all the way out in the parking lot.)

As Joe and Kevin reached the front door, Ann dashed around to the front of the car, and got down on her hands and knees as if she were vomiting.

Joe and Kevin walked towards her and watched her for a few minutes. Kevin kind of edged away. Joe just stood there, about a dozen feet from Ann, with his hands on his hips, looking exasperated.

After a couple of minutes, Kevin walked over to the cable guy's truck and seemed to be watching him assembling his tools.

Joe turned on his heel and returned to their apartment.

As he passed my door, I opened it.

"I think she did that for your benefit," I told Joe.

"Who... Ann?"

"Yes, she was sitting in the car until she heard you two near the front door. Then, she dashed around to the front of the car to make it look like she was sick."

Joe blinked, shrugged, and half grinned. "I'm not surprised."

I nodded in agreement and closed my door.

About five minutes later, I went back to the sofa to get my glass of water from the end table. Joe's car was gone. I expect that he drove Ann to work, where she'll probably continue her performance. Since I'm pretty sure she works at a restaurant, I doubt that they'll let her stay there, but I think this is all about sympathy, anyway.

Henry and Handshake King haven't been back in weeks. If Ann has visitors during the day or early evening, I haven't seen them in the past couple of days. That's a big change. She used to see at least two or three guys, nightly.

I actually feel a little sorry for Ann. She's just a kid, really, and she's already running out of options for a happy life.

Today, I realized that she needs help as much as Kevin and Joe do.

Don't get me wrong. I'm not falling for her obvious "poor me" performance in the parking lot. Maybe she really *was* sick. It's difficult to tell.

The problem is, I'm not convinced she's ready for genuine help, yet.

I'm just thinking about how I'd feel if I were her mother. Right now, Ann should be finishing college and indulging in last-minute summer parties before starting work or grad school.

It seems to me that Ann is badly equipped for normal life. She has a son nearly old enough for kindergarten and a sort-of husband who doesn't seem to care about her. It's sad.

Ann painted herself into this corner, and I don't think she has the *mature* support system she needs to find her way out of this mess. As I said, I don't think she's ready for genuine help. She'll probably keep playing games, acting-out different roles to get the attention that she craves. However, at some point — and I think it'll happen abruptly when it does — she's going to realize that her world has been built on shifting sands.

I hope someone is there when that happens. Throughout this entire story, I've never seen anyone visiting from *Ann's* family. She's mentioned an aunt, and that may be one of the people who picks Ann up (with Ann's laundry), now and then. But, if the aunt has visited Ann at home, I haven't seen her. Generally, the only visitors have been Joe's parents and Henry.

Maybe Ann was a late-in-life child and her parents retired to Florida, but I get the feeling that she's someone without support systems when she desperately needs them. I asked Maryann if she knew whether the family went to church, and she said no. I wish there were *some* other resources I could contact, to get help for Kevin and his parents.

Friday, August 31st, early afternoon

Around 1 PM, I realized that Kevin was playing on the stairs, unsupervised.

It might be different if he was still the kind of child who sits and plays quietly on the landing. He did that when he first moved in, and it didn't worry me.

Now, Kevin jumps from one stair to the next, going downstairs. More than once I've heard him fall, but the flight of stairs is broken by a landing, so Kevin can't fall more than about six feet. When he's fallen, he's never cried or made a noise. He just gets up and goes back to what he was doing.

When he gets bored with the stairs, he races to the top floor and leans over the railing with his stomach on it. That's more worrisome. If he lost his balance up there, he'd fall at least a dozen vertical feet. There is no landing to break his fall, safely.

This afternoon, Kevin was noisy and boisterous. It was kind of a relief after the recent silence that's shrouded his apartment. I wasn't sure if I should just let him play, or encourage him to go back into his apartment.

After a few minutes, I went to the door and looked out.

Kevin glanced back in my direction, raced to his apartment door, opened it, and shouted, "Momma!"

I heard no reply. Kevin looked around, went into the apartment, and closed the door quietly behind him. (That's an unusual gesture for him.)

About 10 minutes later, he was out on the stairs again. By the time I got to the door, he was gone.

A few seconds later, I saw him on the sidewalk outside our apartment, in what looked like pajamas and bare feet. I'm pretty sure Ann was with him, maybe going next door to the building with the washing machines and dryers.

Something's not right. Well, that's how it seems to me.

...

Yes, it *was* a trip to the laundry room. Ann trudged into our building and up the stairs. She was dressed in her usual long-sleeved hoodie outfit with the hood concealing her face. It's 83 degrees outside and considerably warmer on the top floor of our building, where Ann lives. Doesn't she feel how *hot* it is?

Part-way up the stairs, Kevin shouted that he didn't want to go back to the apartment. Ann, just outside my door, shouted at Kevin, "You'd better get up here or I'm going to beat you."

At that moment, it seemed as if everything in

the building went silent. Then, I heard Kevin's sharp intake of breath from downstairs.

I'm sure Ann realized that she'd made a big mistake, using that voice and that language, where the neighbors could hear her.

She hastily changed to her *nice* voice and said, "I'm going to win," as if that was the kind of "beating" she'd been talking about.

By then, Kevin was back at the front door, shouting in a panicky voice, "I don't want you to beat me. Momma, no beating! Don't beat me!"

Ann sighed theatrically and said — still using her nice voice — "You're getting on my nerves. I don't think the neighbors appreciate you shouting."

Kevin continued to plead with her not to beat him.

Ann started down the stairs, sighing and saying, "I don't have time for this." It sounded as if she'd put the clothes basket down on the landing between the first and second floors.

Kevin began to scream. Most of his words ran together, but I could distinguish "don't beat me."

I didn't hear any hitting sounds. Ann's voice was so low, I couldn't hear what she was saying to Kevin, but he suddenly went silent and accompanied her back to their apartment. Through the fish-eye security viewer in my apartment door, I could see her pushing him forward.

Then, everything was quiet in their apartment.

About 10 minutes later — as I'm writing this — Kevin is in his bathroom, screaming, "I don't want to take a shower by myself." The oil painting in my bathroom is rattling because something is hitting Kevin's bathroom wall, hard.

...

I went into my bathroom to see if everything

was okay, and rested one hand on the wall as I straightened the painting. The wall shook, hard, with the next thud from Kevin's apartment.

Kevin shouted, "Stop it!"

Kevin continued to cry, and said something about soap getting in his eyes. Ann shouted back at him, "Suck it up!"

Kevin dissolved into sobs. His words were interrupted with gulps of air, and he said something about not wanting to take a shower by himself. Ann kept telling Kevin he was being stupid, that she didn't have time for this, and he was getting water on the floor. Sometimes, it sounded as if she was in the bathroom. At other times, her voice came from another part of the apartment.

This exchange went on for about three to five minutes, finalized by a loud thud.

I had to walk away. I can't listen to that, and it's done no good to call the police. Ann always has a good excuse for what's going on.

Three rooms away, I can still hear Kevin crying and Ann shouting at Kevin, "Enough! Now!" Every so often, she pauses and shouts loudly, "Quit hitting me!" I'm not sure if that's for the neighbors' benefit, or if Kevin has learned to hit her back.

This behavior is unacceptable, but I feel as if I can't do anything about it.

August 31, late afternoon

When Joe came home from dropping Ann at work, I talked with Joe about getting Kevin involved in sports, especially soccer since Kevin is such a strong kicker.

I explained to Joe that I'd seen newspaper articles about his sports successes in high school. I asked Joe if he'd considered going pro.

Joe said that, during his sophomore year of high school, he'd had a letter asking him to attend a special sports camp. Unfortunately, he was too young to go out-of-state for something like that. Then, by the end of Joe's senior year, Ann was pregnant.

I told Joe that it's not too late. He said yes, but he *felt* old. I reminded him that he's 23, and that's still young.

He paused. Then he said he'd recently received a call from a nearby team. They wanted him to work out with them, to see if he could get back up to speed and play on their team. However, Joe was just promoted to supervisor at his job. He'll be working second shift. That will make it difficult to get to the city where the team practices.

I encouraged Joe to find a way to make the most of this opportunity.

I also asked Joe if he's moving. He said that he is, at the end of September. I asked if he would be taking Kevin with him. He said he couldn't, but he hoped Kevin would join him after a few days.

After that, I told Joe about this diary. I told him I'd do whatever I can to help him keep Kevin safe.

Joe said he might need that. He asked if he should just knock on my door, or what.

I said yes, but if we moved, he could find me online. Especially when I'm working on a book, email can be the fastest way to reach me.

Joe said he doesn't know much about "computer stuff" and the Internet. So, I told him that Maryann, the apartment manager, will know how to reach me. She has my email address.

I've seen Ann using a laptop, and whatever she's doing with her smartphone. (I think she's cruising Facebook and texting.) I've seen Henry using a laptop, too, including the day of the can opener incident in Ann's apartment.

So, I was surprised when Joe said that he doesn't know much about the Internet. For a 23-year-old, that seems odd and kind of sad.

Monday, September 3rd

What's scary is how little I need to say in this update.

1. Ann came home from work around 12:30 AM.

2. She slammed her front door as she entered. That woke me up.

3. Kevin started kicking the wall, rhythmically.

4. Ann went into his room. I heard the usual overlapping thuds and mostly unintelligible shouts. They occurred between 12:46 AM (when I looked at the clock) and 1:30 AM.

The variations from what I usually hear:

1. After Ann entered the room and started talking to him in a low voice, Kevin started shouting "Daddy!" Then, for the next half hour or so, Kevin seemed silent. All I heard were intermittent bouts of overlapping thuds and slapping sounds, and an occasional sound similar to Ann's voice. Then, towards the end of the hour, Kevin started shouting angrily, "Momma! No!"

2. When Kevin began shouting "No!" Ann yelled back, "Stop hitting me!" She did that last week, too. I'm not convinced that Kevin is actually hitting Ann. I think she's shouting that for the neighbors (including me) to hear.

I think Ann came home angry, as usual. However, it sounded as if Kevin made sure he got attention by kicking the wall. That's troubling.

I also think Kevin is old enough to start *resisting* what Ann is doing. I'm not sure that he's hitting back, but things *are* changing.

Tuesday, September 4th

Today, Ann and Kevin were visited by a blond woman carrying a magenta plastic file folder. I hope she was from DHHS Child Protective Services.

I wouldn't have known that she was there, except that Kevin was fussy at the apartment door when she was leaving. He didn't want her to go.

She calmed him by telling him to go to the balcony and wave to her, and she'd wave back.

Kevin and Ann had an argument after the blond woman left. It wasn't huge, and I didn't hear any slapping or thuds, just a normal argument.

(I re-read that and realize how weird it sounds. No mother should have a "normal argument" with a four-year-old. Parenting should never reach that level... not *normally*, anyway.)

Wednesday, September 5th

It sounds as if Kevin is throwing himself against his apartment door. The noise is so loud, I wasn't sure if someone was pounding on *my* front door.

I heard five loud thuds after that, and Ann shouting something. (I'm not sure what it was. She was trying to talk over the thuds.)

I walked away after making sure no one was pounding on our door. I'm attending an important webinar at 3 PM, and I can't stop my work *every* time Ann and Kevin create a scene.

Thursday, September 7th

Yesterday afternoon, Kevin was throwing

himself against his front door, again. I have no idea what's going on, inside that apartment, and why he's not covered with bruises from doing this.

Ann was, as usual, yelling at him as he was hitting the door. Her words were unintelligible, but I could vaguely make out Kevin's name.

This particular door-ramming session lasted about 30 seconds.

Then, around 9 PM last night, Joe came home from work.

Ordinarily, Ann and Joe leave their apartment door unlocked. I suppose they figure this is a low-crime area or something.

Anyway, yet again, I thought someone was knocking at my door. No, it was Joe, knocking *on his own door.*

Not a sound came from his apartment. After a couple of minutes, Joe stopped knocking and trudged downstairs, out to his car. I watched from my window. His shoulders were even more slumped than usual. If there were illustrations for "defeated man" in the dictionary, his photo would be there.

Around the time that Joe got to his car, Kevin must have seen him through the apartment window, too.

I heard shouting as Kevin ripped open the door and ran into the hall, shrieking at the top of his lungs. "Daddy, come back! We're here, Daddy! Don't go!"

This went on for about 20 seconds — which seemed like an eternity — as Ann dragged Kevin back into the apartment. She commanded Kevin to quiet down. Then, Ann told Kevin that Joe wasn't there.

Kevin started crying hysterically, insisting that he *had* seen his daddy. Ann bellowed back that he hadn't. She insisted he was making it up.

By the time I got to the patio to get Joe's attention, he was pulling out of the parking lot. He didn't see me.

This tells me two things: Sometimes, when people knock at the door, Ann pretends not to be at home. She must have gotten Kevin to play along with this. Otherwise, Kevin would have responded when Joe knocked.

And, Ann must have deliberately locked the door to keep Joe out. She knew when Joe was due home from work, and she wasn't going to let him in.

At some point last night, Joe returned and — since his car is now in the parking lot — he probably got into the apartment.

I feel sorry for Joe, but I'm even more distressed that Kevin is in the middle of this. And, even worse, Ann told Kevin that he was wrong and Daddy wasn't there, when Kevin *certainly* saw him.

That's not only cruel to Kevin, but it's the kind of thing that makes a kid doubt his grasp of reality. He *knew* he'd seen his dad, but his mom said he *didn't*.

I may try calling DHHS again. I'm not sure that I'll make any progress, and I feel kind of numb about that. Still, I have to make *some* effort to rouse the state to help Kevin.

I'm starting to put this diary into book format. This information, in the right hands, *might* bring attention to Kevin's situation. It may help reveal how badly the system fails some families. Mostly, with the election coming up, I hope this book might attract more attention than it would at another time of year.

Wednesday, September 12th

Kevin is throwing himself against the inside of his apartment door, again.

How can I tell that he's doing this himself, and Ann isn't abusing him? That's easy to explain: Kevin's noises are different.

Kevin does things *rhythmically*. I've mentioned that before. Kevin's rhythmic noises are so consistent, either he's going to be a musician or there may be an autism link there.

On the other hand, Ann simply acts-out. It sounds like a flurry of anger, and sometimes uncontrolled rage. Though I believe some of her behaviors are rooted in compulsion, she doesn't do things the rhythmic way that Kevin does.

The current slams against the apartment door aren't quite rhythmic, but close enough, so I'm pretty sure it's Kevin, acting-out. I hear very little fussing. Also, Kevin's body doesn't slide down as it does when he's thrown against his bedroom wall. So, I think he's doing this himself.

Earlier this week, I heard drama in Kevin's bedroom. I'm not sure if it was Monday night or Tuesday night. I can't believe I'm that jaded about it, at this point... but I am.

I heard lots of crying that sounded like Kevin, and Ann yelling at him. It went on for about half an hour, I think. After a while, I quit checking the clock. I drifted in and out of sleep, mostly annoyed because — with three fans and the window a/c running in our bedroom — I shouldn't hear our neighbors at *all*.

I didn't hear any slaps or thuds, so I'm not sure if that qualifies as abuse. That's why I didn't even add it to this journal, when it happened.

In my opinion, Kevin's behavior issues aren't helped by Ann waking him up when she comes home from work. Whether she's just yelling at him or hitting him, it's still abuse and it's a bad habit.

But hey, what do I know? I haven't seen DHHS return, so maybe Ann's parenting skills were deemed adequate.

Yes, I'm feeling frustrated and bitter today. I get cranky when I'm woken up, night after night. It's been too long since I could go to bed without worrying that I'd be woken by someone screaming, sometimes less than a dozen feet away.

Thursday, September 13th

Yesterday, Kevin had a second bout of throwing himself at the door, about half an hour after my previous post.

Then, late in the afternoon — shortly before 4 PM — I was in the shower. Suddenly, I could hear a cacophony of screams and shouts, including Ann's signature nails-on-the-chalkboard screeching.

By the time I got to my door and looked out, I could see Ann carrying Kevin. Joe's dad was in the hall, waiting for her. Kevin was writhing and wriggling, trying to get away from her, and he screamed something about wanting to watch TV.

Ann yelled back at him — her face no more than 18 inches from his — that he had to go outside with her.

Joe's dad kept saying, "C'mon, Kevin, let's go."

Ann emerged from the apartment, did a very *fake* stumble, and held Kevin — still squirming — over the railing. If she dropped him, he'd fall about 15 or 20 feet (two half-flights of stairs, with a landing in-between) to the floor below. Then Ann shouted, "Quit it or you're going to fall all the way down there."

I'm sure it was *supposed* to look as if Kevin's writhing had thrown her off-balance. It would have been more convincing if she hadn't paused, with Kevin dangling over the railing, a split second too long.

(Kevin is four years old, so I'm not sure *why* I flashed on that picture of Michael Jackson, holding his infant son over the side of his balcony.)

Did Joe's father recognize what Ann was doing, and how dangerous it was for Kevin? I don't know, but Joe's dad insisted on taking Kevin from Ann. Then, Joe's dad carried Kevin downstairs, himself.

All the way down the stairs, Kevin kept screaming, "I want to stay with Momma!"

That's baffling. Really, if someone treated *me* the way I've seen and heard her treat Kevin, I'd be eager to get away from her.

What is going on...?

I remember when Ann called the police to report Kevin for being badly behaved. According to Maryann, Ann told Kevin that if he didn't behave after that, she'd have the police lock Kevin up.

I'm wondering what kind of threats Ann is feeding Kevin now. I'm *sure* she knows that Joe is leaving her in about two weeks. I expect that she's preparing for the court scene, when the judge might ask Kevin which parent he wants to live with.

However, Ann doesn't seem to *like* Kevin very much. I've seen no affection at all. At best, it looks as if Ann thinks he's a nuisance she has to tolerate. I'd be astonished if she wants custody of Kevin, unless she's counting on a hefty amount of child support. Of course, Ann would use most of the money for herself.

Meanwhile, it looks as if Ann has made another

attempt at dying her hair blond. Or maybe pink. It's so splotchy in the back, it's difficult to tell. She's also really skinny again.

Most of the neighbors know what's ahead when Ann is in a really skinny phase.

For the next day or two, she'll spend much of the day on her balcony. We'll see her smoking with shaky hands, waiting for a friend to meet her in the parking lot. Everything will be fine for a few hours after that, maybe even for a day or two. Then Ann will be back on the balcony again, smoking and looking anxious. Even if Kevin is right next to her, trying to get her attention, it's as if she doesn't know he's there.

This cycle has repeated itself so many times during the past year, it's pretty much a sure thing.

Today, there was another scene. A little before 5 PM, Ann and Kevin were back. That surprised me. I hadn't seen them return after Joe's dad's visit, but I wasn't really watching, either.

This time, Ann left with Kevin and three bags of laundry, in a shiny silver Toyota. Kevin didn't want to go out, but — this time — Ann didn't have to yell or pick him up. Kevin walked out on his own.

Ann left a big note on her door. I'm sure she expected at least one neighbor to read it, and — of course — I did. Her note said that she'd gone to her aunt's to do laundry, and Joe should pick them up after he got home. She signed it, "Love ya," followed by her name.

The weird thing is, there's a perfectly nice laundry room in our building. Not long ago, they installed new, front-loading washing machines.

In addition, there's a great laundromat less than a block away, and the weather has been lovely.

But, hey, maybe Ann can't afford the two or

three dollars it'd cost to use the laundry room.

The note confirms that Ann *has* an aunt, so she's not without relatives who could help.

Meanwhile, Ann's interactions with Kevin — versus Joe's time with him — have been on my mind lately.

Except for two incidents this summer, I've never seen Ann treat Kevin as if she's a loving mother. The first time was when Ann said she was babysitting. Then, there were a couple of times when she and Joe put on a big show of playing with water guns. Except for those episodes — each less than 30 minutes or so — I have *never* seen Ann take Kevin outside for anything *fun*. Not for a walk, or to play in the field directly in front of our building.

On the other hand, until Joe started working second shift, he used to take Kevin outside to play in the field. It might have been once a week or once every two weeks, but he played outside with Kevin as a normal parent would.

These days, Ann is almost always at home. Surely, she could walk down the stairs and across the parking lot to the nearby field, to play ball or Frisbee with Kevin, now and then.

Friday, September 14th

At about 4 PM, Ann was leaving for work. (I was surprised to see her in her waitstaff uniform. I thought she'd been fired again.)

Kevin's grandmother had arrived to give Ann a lift, and I think she was going to babysit Kevin. However, Kevin put up another fight. Ann kept shoving Kevin as he walked downstairs. I could see them through the security viewer in my door. She pushed him forward at the top of the stairs, and I heard her continue to push him, step by step, all the way to the first floor.

The stairs are steep and narrow. I wondered if Ann *wanted* Kevin to fall.

Then, as soon as Ann secured Kevin in the back seat of his grandmother's car, Ann went back to her apartment for her backpack. Kevin was back upstairs just a few seconds after her.

Another argument ensued. He wanted some handheld game. Ann went back into the apartment and got it, but then waved it just above Kevin's reach, telling him he couldn't have it until he got into the car.

That's a reasonable way to get a child to do what you want, but the way she did it, *taunting* Kevin... it bothered me a little.

She's a young mother. With experience, I hope she'll learn to be kinder.

Friday, September 21st, 8:10 AM

The week had been quiet. I'd been woken by noises in Kevin's room a few times, but nothing significant. I don't pay much attention when it sounds as if Kevin is throwing toys against the wall, or playing.

Then, yesterday afternoon, I heard scuffling sounds from Kevin's apartment, off and on. They weren't enough to get me out of my chair where I was working.

I didn't hear Ann and Kevin leaving at the usual time, either, so I guess Ann had another day off.

However, around 5 PM, I heard a really loud crack. Something hard must have hit the front door of Kevin's apartment.

I got up and looked out, but the hall was completely silent. Not a sound followed for the next minute or so, and I went back to my home office to work.

Then, around 8:50 PM when Joe came home from work, all *Hades* broke loose. I heard Kevin shouting, then Ann bellowing back. If Joe was saying anything, his voice was subdued. (When there's an argument in that apartment, I only hear Ann's voice, never Joe's.)

After that, I heard the water running in their bathroom, and Kevin was whining and probably kicking things. There were lots of thuds, but not as if Kevin was being hit... just quick bumps on the walls and the occasional thud around the toilet area.

That lasted about 30 minutes, off and on. My guess...? Joe wanted Kevin to have a bath or shower before bedtime, but Ann hadn't been up to it. Kevin was tired and cranky and put up a fuss.

An argument that lasts that long... maybe I *should* have expected more to follow, but I really thought the ruckus was over for the night.

Everything seemed fine after that, or at least I wasn't woken by it until 4:30 this morning. It sounded as if Kevin was crying, loudly. That's an interesting thing about Kevin: He hardly ever simply *cries*. He's either whining or he's in a rage, shouting while crying. There's no in-between.

This morning, it sounded like a tragic wail, not Kevin's usual angry outburst.

About 10 minutes later, Kevin started his usual rhythmic kicking. I'm pretty sure he was on his back in his bed, kicking the wall. It's always so rhythmic, I can usually drift back to sleep.

In this case, I couldn't. Kevin stopped kicking. His cries grew louder and sadder. Then I heard Ann. Her voice was different, too. It was higher-pitched. She sounded more frantic and frustrated. As usual, I couldn't distinguish her words.

Then, I heard the overlapping thuds, and Kevin

shouted "No!" five or six times. Ann's voice was muted, but she was saying something.

After that, I heard the thuds but no voices, and — after about 10 minutes — all was quiet again.

The crying-arguing-thud sequence woke me two more times. Then, around 5:30 AM, Kevin seemed to reach the snapping point again. I heard him clearly shout, "No! Momma! Stop! Stop! Stop! Momma, stop!"

Sleep was impossible, so I got up and called the police.

I have no illusions about the police actually *hearing* what's going on, or being able to do anything about it. After all, Ann is going to tell the police a good story. Joe will back her up. Kevin — fearful that the police will take him to jail if he doesn't behave the way Ann wants him to — won't say anything revealing.

So, calling the police is pretty pointless.

However, I want Ann to know that we neighbors *are* aware of what's going on. We hear her with Kevin and we suspect child abuse.

So, I call the police anyway.

The problem is, at least *one* police officer seems to think the whole thing is a joke. Each time he shows up, the routine is predictable.

First, the officer knocks on Ann's door. She opens it for him, and says something very quietly. It's her throaty voice. He laughs. Ann jokes with him some more. Together, they walk towards Kevin's bedroom.

A few minutes later, the officer leaves, still chuckling. Ann smiles and flirts with him. He blushes and laughs again, saying that she should call if she needs anything else. Then, he walks down the stairs and out the door.

My husband witnessed this exchange, tonight, and he was livid. One reason we'd chosen this apartment complex was because we'd be living near a police station. Between *this* kind of response to a call, to the fact that Handshake King seemed pretty open about setting up shop in the parking lot, I'm becoming increasingly uneasy about living here.

And, oh yes, there's the registered sex offender in the next building — with *two* counts of sex crimes — but I can't think about that now.

Mostly, I am so *very* tired of being woken in the middle of the night by screams, shouts, cries, and thuds in Kevin's bedroom, and the sound of Ann yelling at Kevin.

It's been nearly a year since I first heard slaps and thuds in the middle of the night, and Kevin screaming for help.

I'm beginning to think that the *only* way to deal with this is to move away. There is *no* help for Kevin or his parents. Not from what I've seen, so far.

Friday, 4:32 PM

I am so disgusted right now, I can barely see straight. This situation is completely insane, and *I played right into it.*

Four times in the past hour, Kevin has escaped from his apartment.

I say "escaped" because — each time — he runs out, wearing only his underpants. Then, he dashes downstairs. The problem is, when he gets to the front walk, he doesn't know what to do. He pauses. He's outside so rarely, I doubt that he knows where to go for help.

Today, a young man is visiting Ann. His license plates are from Massachusetts. I don't think I've seen him before. Sometimes, next door is a revolving door of men, especially when Joe isn't at home. But, sometimes it's the same when Joe *is* there, but (apparently) asleep.

Anyway, each time Kevin gets out of the building, Ann has *eventually* gone down the stairs, in her hoodie and huge, wrap-around sunglasses. But, her response time is amazingly slow.

Five minutes later:

Make that *five* times that Kevin has escaped. Right now, he's outside, balancing on his toes — tightrope-style — on the wall by the front door. He's wearing underpants, and that's all.

I'm not sure where Ann is. I can hear her voice. Her apartment door is open, but I don't know if she's outside, or inside the building, on the stairs, or what.

The first three times today, Ann went after Kevin and carried him most of the way upstairs. The third time he escaped, I heard her on the stairs telling Kevin, "Do what you're told or I'll call the cops and they'll take you away." She put him down and he ran upstairs, slamming the door.

The fourth time, Kevin got as far as my door. That's when Ann shouted after him, "I'm calling." He paused and looked back. Ann held her cell phone up for him to see, and it looked as if she was entering a phone number.

Kevin shouted, "No!" Then, he ran back into the apartment, shouting that she's mean.

So, I played right into her game. Kevin *knows* the police were there this morning. Now, Ann is making it sound as if they were there to... I don't know... does Kevin *really* think they'd take him to jail?

5 minutes after that:

I called DHHS a few minutes ago. The central intake office gave me the *current* caseworker's name and her regional office phone number. I called that office... and they're closed for the day.

It's Friday. This means I can't reach them until Monday.

It seems to me that there should be *someone* I can call, *at least 9 to 5,* daily. I'm *not* equipped to determine what's an emergency in this kind of situation.

I've left messages with DHHS in the past. No one has ever returned my call. I have no idea which neighbors still care enough to report the situation, but I suspect that — for the past month (or longer) — I've been the only one reporting Ann's abuse to the police and DHHS.

Today, it's not a *life-and-death* emergency. I'm not comfortable calling the police, especially since Ann will turn that to her advantage. I'm also tired of calling them and, by the time they get here, everything seems normal again.

Lately, there have been bigger crimes at our apartment complex, including burglaries and car thefts from our parking lot. The police have enough to do, without getting called to an apartment where nothing criminal seems to be going on.

I'm *tired.* I've been dealing with anguish, frustration, and sleep deprivation for most of the past year, and — looking at this situation — I feel as if I'm Scarlett O'Hara, saying, "I'll think about that tomorrow."

I'm worn down. I don't know what to do.

Tuesday, September 25th

Tonight, at the Best Buy near our home, I saw Kevin with Joe. They looked happy, and I was glad to see them, too. It gave me a chance to tell Joe that calling the police had apparently played into Ann's plans, again, and that Kevin was afraid of them.

As if on cue, Kevin announced, "Yeah, the cops will take you away if you scream too much."

I corrected Kevin, and Joe did, too. I explained that the police *won't* do that, and Kevin didn't need to be afraid of them. Kevin looked at me as if he didn't believe me.

Before I left them, I told Kevin that if he ever needs help, he can knock on my door and — if I'm at home — I'll help him.

I hope he remembers that.

Wednesday, September 26th

This morning, Kevin knocked at my door. Ann was watching him from her doorway.

Kevin looked up at me as if he wasn't sure what to say. Then, he glanced back at Ann.

I was surprised to see her. She's packing on the pounds again, and her eyes seemed to bulge slightly. She announced, "He said you told him he could knock at your door if he needed help."

I said yes. Then I asked Kevin if he needed help.

He nodded yes, and glanced cautiously back at Ann, and shifted his weight from foot to foot. He looked at the floor and twisted his hands a little. Then he said his poop was orange and brown.

I thanked him for letting me know. I asked if there was anything else he needed to tell me.

Again, Kevin glanced warily back at Ann.

She announced, "He fell off the back of the couch," as if that was supposed to explain something.

Then she said, "C'mon, buddy, that's enough now."

Kevin looked up at me with a worried expression. After a couple of seconds, he shrugged dramatically and followed Ann back to their apartment.

Saturday, September 29th

Late yesterday morning, Kevin began kicking the wall rhythmically. That went on, all day and past 8:30 PM (when I fell asleep), interrupted only by shouting matches with Ann.

At 12:04 AM this morning, it sounded as if a tornado was turned loose in Kevin's bedroom. I think it started with him shouting and throwing things, fairly rhythmically, at the walls.

Then, I heard Ann's voice shouting over him, followed by silence. The next sound was lots of slapping. I have no idea if Ann was slapping Kevin or vice versa, but... wow, that was impressive. It sounded as if a full-on battle being waged. Nobody shouted or cried. In fact, I didn't hear a word. I still don't know what was going on.

It wasn't as loud as the usual outbursts, so I drifted off to sleep about 20 minutes later.

As of 8:00 this morning, there's no sound from their apartment. However, if Joe holds firm to his promise, he'll move out this weekend.

Joe won't be here to pay the rent on Monday, and Ann will be evicted.

This may be a buckle-your-seatbelts series of days and nights, unless Joe backs down from his decision to move out.

I'm not convinced Joe will go through with this. It's a pretty gutsy move for a guy who's so soft-spoken and subdued.

Sunday, September 30th, early morning

Yesterday, it was difficult to cling to hope. Instead of seeing Joe move his belongings, I saw him go out with Kevin, then return, and then go out with both Ann and Kevin, smiling and laughing. Once again, they seemed to be a model family.

I want them to get along. I *want* them to be responsible parents. But, even at their best, Joe hasn't been able to prevent the middle-of-the-night screaming and other sounds. He needs to move out — on his own, if necessary — and then start the legal gears turning to get full custody.

Meanwhile, Ann has yet another hair color, and she's ironing it straight, too. That's a *really* bad sign. Ann's hairstyle changes usually indicate another personality shift.

Yesterday morning, every time I went out, I glanced up at Ann's balcony. Each time, she was squatting in the door frame, smoking. She reminded me of one of those little gray gargoyle figurines sold around Halloween. I know she was trying to keep the smoke outside (away from the smoke detector) but remain indoors enough to stay warm, but still... it looked very odd.

During the afternoon, my husband and I ran errands. When we returned, Kevin ran down the stairs to meet us. He was in a tee shirt and underpants. Kevin paused and seemed to be studying my expression. He looked panicky but didn't say anything. I noticed that his right eye was swollen, and he had a purple bruise on the brow bone, about the size of a dime.

Then, Kevin ran downstairs to where my husband was bringing in groceries.

Kevin shouted up to Ann, saying he needed some cool air. Ann shouted back that he needed to put on more clothes first.

About a minute or two later, Kevin ran back up the stairs, carrying two toys. One was a mask of some kind.

By then, Ann was at her front door. She said,

"Hey, buddy, those aren't your toys."

Kevin replied, "No, but I want them."

Ann told Kevin that he needed to put them back. He said he didn't want to.

Then she said, "Well, okay, but if anyone comes looking for those toys, you'll have to give them back."

Kevin agreed and went into his apartment, carrying the toys proudly.

So, Kevin learned that it's *okay* to take other people's things, as long as they don't know you have them.

Everything was quiet for the rest of the day.

Then, at 12:46 AM (this morning), I was woken by long, extended screaming. It was Kevin's voice. Each was at least three seconds long, and in a higher range — in terms of pitch and volume — than his usual. In between, I heard Kevin shouting, "Help! Daddy!" and "Momma, stop hitting!" plus other things I couldn't understand. His voice was shrill.

I also heard the usual, layered thud-on-thud sounds, plus a new one. I'm pretty sure it was another neighbor, hitting the wall or ceiling with something, protesting the noise.

The noise was *so* startling and awful, I ran out of the bedroom. On my way out the door, I shouted to my husband, "I'm calling the police. This is unacceptable."

As my husband later pointed out, Ann certainly heard me.

By the time the police officer arrived, Ann was ready. He'd barely rapped once on the door when she opened it and said cheerfully, "Yeah, c'mon in," followed by a theatrical sigh.

A few minutes later, the officer left. I'm not sure that there was anything for him to see. I wished I'd had the presence of mind to mention the swelling and bruise over Kevin's right eye. But, surely, the officer had studied Kevin closely, looking for evidence of abuse...?

I called Maryann and left a message. I don't think I've ever called her at such a late hour, but Kevin's terror was so extreme, I was worried.

September 30th, late morning

Early last week, I visited one of the new neighbors who'd mentioned noises she heard. She'd said were coming from Kevin's apartment.

So, I'd explained what *I* thought was going on, and asked her to call the police if she heard anything that might be child abuse.

She agreed. Until I spoke with her, she thought Kevin was just a badly behaved child.

Well, Kevin *is* a badly behaved child. I'm sure he needs medical care for his hyperactivity.

She had a few stories of her own, such as incidents of Kevin urinating from the balcony. I'm not sure where Ann was at the time, but it's another vivid symptom of a neglected child.

The neighbor is an older woman, but definitely feisty. I liked her spirit when we talked. She seemed like someone with a lot of energy, and a strong sense of right and wrong. It was a relief to find someone who understood.

When I left the neighbor's apartment, I felt certain that she'd do the right thing if she was woken by Ann abusing Kevin.

I just want people to call the police if they hear something that's not right.

I have witnessed Kevin's neglect. I've heard Ann threaten to hit or beat Kevin, and I've heard her threaten to hit Henry. So, I'm pretty sure she's the abuser I'm hearing in Kevin's room at night. But, to be honest, I don't have x-ray vision. I could be wrong.

The *real* issue is Kevin's safety, and getting him the help he needs. That's best done by professionals. The only way *they'll* get involved is after enough credible reports by multiple neighbors who hear the late-night noises.

So, this morning, after I returned home from church, I visited that same neighbor. I was *certain* she'd heard last night's noises.

I asked her if she'd heard anything. She said, "Well...," and paused.

Her nephew interrupted, and said that he'd heard "the kid" during the night. Then the nephew shouted as he jumped up and down, demonstrating what "the kid" had been doing.

I glanced back at the aunt. She looked uncomfortable with her nephew's demonstration. So, I said to her, "You heard the screaming, too, right?"

She looked away, paused, and said something I didn't understand.

I repeated my question and she said, "Well, yes..."

Still lots of avoidance. What happened to her, since we talked before? Where was the spark... the feisty attitude? It's as if I was talking with her apathetic, subdued twin sister.

I asked if she'd called the police. Silence. Then, she glanced at the front door, saying, "That young woman... she's very troubled."

"So, you didn't call the police."

Suddenly, the aunt seemed very interested in her hands. She wouldn't look at me. Then she said, "Well... no."

She continued sitting on the edge of her chair, looking down at her hands, wringing them slightly. I felt like I was in Stepford. Frankly, her personality shift was kind of creepy, but maybe that's how interrupted sleep affected *her*. I don't know.

After a few minutes of uncomfortable silence, I thanked her for her time and left. I felt *very* frustrated.

If neighbors won't get involved when they're aware of problems, *the abuse will continue*. I can't be the *only* person calling the police when Kevin is screaming for help. It makes me look like a 21st century version of Alice Kravitz. That's *not* the role I had in mind.

So, do I throw in the towel, figuring I can't change anything, or what...?

Rhetorical question.

What I'm doing is working on this book. Nothing else has helped, so far, but I'll make one more effort.

Then, with all of my calls and reports to the police, DHHS, and Joe's family, *and* this story in the hands of people who *can* make a difference, I'll have done my best to help Kevin.

But, there's a bigger issue. This book is about *the lack of functioning systems* to assess and get help to families that need it the most.

I printed out several key pages from my diary and sent them to the caseworker at DHHS. I included an annotated calendar from August. The calendar gives a quick, visual overview of the problems in Kevin's home. I hope that helps.

I showed some of the pages to Maryann. She wanted to copy them for Joe's mom, but I don't want to risk a scene that could cause Ann to bolt with Kevin. In the past, she's threatened to do that.

I told Maryann that she can *tell* Joe's mom about this diary. Once Joe has moved out and Kevin is out of danger, I might print the important parts of this and give Maryann a copy. What she does with it... that's up to her.

Unless Joe has been keeping a diary himself, my records are the best way to show a judge what's been going on in Kevin's home for the past year.

Knowing this exists, I'm *hoping* Joe has the courage to leave Ann and take Kevin with him. I don't think Joe understands how clear the contrasts are between his behavior and Ann's. Unless there's something I don't know, gaining custody shouldn't be difficult for Joe.

- Joe is the former high school sports hero who's had a steady job ever since he moved in here.

- He's the soft-spoken guy whose voice I've never heard raised, when talking with Kevin.

- He's the one who takes Kevin outside to play, something I've never seen Ann do, except the *one* day she said she was babysitting.

- He's the one who's never threatened to hit or beat Kevin... not that I heard, anyway.

- If Joe has ever brought another woman to his apartment, the way Ann welcomes men when Joe isn't there... well, I've never seen it.

To me, this seems a simple decision for any judge. Of the two, Joe looks appears to be the *far* more stable, responsible parent.

I've told Joe that, if he needs me to go to court with him, I will. Maryann has said the same thing.

September 30th, later

When I returned to my apartment, voicemail was waiting for me. It was Maryann. She said Joe was still planning to move and take Kevin with him. Joe's family and support system were ready to make this as easy as possible for everyone.

Maryann said she'd told Joe to have a police officer on hand, as both a witness and to keep the peace. Maryann wasn't convinced that Joe would take that precaution, so she asked me to call the police if — during Joe's move — I heard or saw anything alarming.

I agreed.

Within 48 hours, all of this should be concluded.

If Ann remains in the apartment, that's fine with me. The issue is Kevin's safety. Knowing that Joe is taking Kevin away from Ann's cruelty... that's going to be a relief.

I've never been 100% sure that Joe wasn't part of the problem. However, if he finally takes steps to get help for his son, that's enough to give me peace of mind.

Monday, October 1st, morning

If Joe moved out yesterday, it must have been after 9:30 PM.

I saw Joe leave his apartment late yesterday afternoon, but he wasn't carrying *anything*. He got into his car. Then, he drove away.

Ann and Kevin left about 15 minutes later. They were in a red car driven by a young woman.

Ann and the young woman returned, later in the day. Shortly after that, Joe and Kevin arrived, together.

But, when I went to bed, nothing had changed. I saw no evidence that Joe was actually moving out.

I'm pretty sure the woman in the red car is the same one Ann has called in the past, when she's had an argument with Joe. It's what Ann does when she wants to make amends with Joe.

The routine is always the same: When Ann opens the apartment door, the woman practically shimmies in. Her laugh is low as she walks directly towards Joe. I see him smile, and I see

Ann studying his reaction. Ann's face is usually expressionless. Then, she quietly closes the door.

I don't *think* it's Joe's sister, but — hey — maybe it's a really close family. In the past, during the mornings *following* the arrival of this woman, Joe always had a spring in his step as he walks to his car.

In other words, nothing would surprise me this morning.

But, tawdry or not, what goes on in private — between consenting adults — is none of my business. And, when the woman in the red car spends the night, Kevin usually seems to sleep, undisturbed.

This time was different. I *did* hear noises from Kevin's bedroom.

I was woken around 2:30 AM by something that sounded as if dresser drawers were being slammed. That seemed odd. I've never heard dresser noises from Kevin's room. I'd assumed that he didn't have one, but maybe — until now — it hadn't occurred to him to slam the drawers.

When I got up in the morning, Joe's car was gone. My husband said he heard Joe leave around 6.

Right now, the red car is still in the parking lot.

I *hope* Joe and Kevin moved out during the night, and the woman with the red car was there as emotional support for Ann. I'd like to be really, *really* wrong about what was going on, when the woman showed up yesterday.

Kevin deserves to be in a home where people truly care about him. I don't see much evidence that Ann has any emotional connection with Kevin.

And, to be frank: I *really* need an uninterrupted night's sleep.

October 1st, later

This afternoon, Joe, his dad, and a friend loaded Joe's furniture and personal belongings into the back of a pickup truck.

I should have had more faith in Joe. I feel silly for doubting his resolve. I still have questions about Joe, but at least he did what he said: He moved out, and took Kevin with him.

Yes, Kevin was in the pickup truck as it pulled out of the driveway, a few minutes ago.

Ann was in the driveway, saying goodbye. If there was any drama, it was quiet. No tears. She didn't even look upset as she walked back towards our building. If anything, she looked relieved and a little thoughtful.

This story is far from concluded, but it's time to close this diary and get back to a normal life. It's been a long time since I've had a good night's sleep.

Ann may have a temper tantrum tonight, but it won't involve her son. That's a relief.

I can't claim that this is a *happy* ending to the story, but it's a better outcome than I'd expected.

I want Kevin and *all* children to have happy lives, living in homes where they feel loved and safe. That's why I'm publishing this story, hoping it makes an impact on people who can make a difference.

The system is overburdened. Resources need to be reorganized so neighbors who suspect abuse can report it. *Every* case must be fully assessed. Communities need to examine local resources — churches, help lines, etc. — so the burden isn't solely on the police and the government.

I'm not sure what the answer is. I'm certain it's not a simple solution.

For me, this has been an excruciating year, but

I believe that Kevin is safe with his dad now. That's what matters.

There are *other* Kevins, in New Hampshire and other states, and some of them are in far worse situations than I witnessed.

When a neighbor *repeatedly* reports what seems like child abuse and neglect, there must be resources — several of them — so no *other* Kevins fall through the cracks.

Tuesday, October 2nd

If someone had told me how exhausted and stressed I'd become over the past year, due to sleep deprivation, I'd have moved out as soon as Ann moved in. The effects were gradual, insidious, and damaging. I'm sure they impacted my mental health and decision-making abilities, as well as my work and family relationships.

But, that's over now. Kevin is safe, and Ann is alone, next door.

Around 2 AM, I heard a single, very loud thud next door. It sounded as if a dresser had been pushed over. That was probably Ann's temper tantrum.

I knew it wasn't Kevin. I didn't even look at the clock, but went back to sleep immediately. Then, I slept more soundly than I have in so long, I can't even put a time frame on it.

The "ah-HA!" for me is: Though I was *fully* awake for the sounds of abuse I reported in my diary, something was probably disturbing my sleep almost *every* night. It just wasn't loud enough for me to be fully conscious of it.

This morning, I'm even *more* relieved that Kevin is away from Ann, and — I hope — able to begin sleeping soundly at night, himself.

My questions about Joe's role increase as I

reflect on the events of the past year. However, Kevin's well-being is now in the hands of the court system. I'm trusting them to look into every aspect of this, and make appropriate decisions.

I'll bounce back after a few more nights of uninterrupted sleep.

For Kevin, who's probably been dealing with this his entire *life,* the process may be more gradual. I don't envy Joe's challenges. It's going to time and Joe will need patience while Kevin unwinds from abuse and learns to live a normal life. I hope Joe has the support network he needs, and that Kevin gets the counseling he'll need.

Today, I'm editing my diary entries to turn them into a book. It's election season in the U.S., and I'll be sharing this book with every candidate and elected official who might be able to make a difference. I'm not sure that anyone will pay attention, but it's worth a try.

I wish I'd been able to get help for Kevin, sooner, but at least he's in his father's care, now.

Maybe this story can help others. I hope so.

Why I Published this Book

For me, this story is about the increasing isolation of people within communities. It's also about neighbors who didn't want to get involved.

It reveals the faulty mindset of a society — including me — that expects others to take responsibility for social and family problems.

We're expecting laws and government offices to fix what's wrong, but we don't make sure they're *able* to do their jobs. Whether it's a legal, financial, staff, or oversight problem, we expect to drop the issue on the shoulders of someone else, and have it fully handled *with no further efforts from us.*

Obviously, that doesn't always work.

Personal responsibility is the answer, and the only one we can rely on.

That doesn't absolve anyone from reporting incidents of suspected child abuse or neglect. In New Hampshire, it's the law.

According to the DHHS website, "**NH Law** requires **any person** who **suspects** that a child under age 18 has been abused or neglected **must report** that suspicion immediately to DCYF." (Emphasis per that website.)

Initially, I threw this together into a Kindle book because the 2012 elections were imminent. I knew I could make the book free for five days, so I did. Then, I contacted every elected official and candidate in NH who seemed like he or she might read this... and for whom I had an email address.

One candidate contacted me after reading the book. No one else did.

I also sent printed copy of key chapters from this book to the NH office that handles child abuse cases. And, I sent them the link to the free book as well. (Their response: They said they had no reports of child abuse from anyone named Shannon Bowen. That's despite the fact that I gave them my real name and Kevin's real name, when I contacted them.)

Mostly, I published Kevin's story to highlight the importance of effective abuse prevention, intervention, and recovery resources at the federal, state, and community levels.

From my viewpoint, the police would *like* to help, but laws prevent them from protecting children except in cases of the most flagrant, public abuse.

The DHHS staff would *like* to help, but they're overwhelmed with cases and hampered by the same laws that prevent the police from intervening.

The NH governor's office would *like* to help, but "right to privacy" laws prevent them from accessing DHHS files. Oversight and accountability are limited.

So, I compiled this book and published it, hoping to attract attention to a growing problem among overstressed families and systems.

Though this book has been an Amazon best-seller in its category, I never expected the global attention Kevin's story has received. Although many readers are highly critical of what I did (and didn't do), I'm tremendously grateful to those who understand the dilemma I faced, and have left heartfelt comments and reviews of this book.

What's True in this Book

The major events in this story are true. Everything took place in New Hampshire between November 2011 and October 2012.

Remember: In this book, *all* names, descriptions, and locations have been changed to conceal the identities of the individuals. No one involved is *actually* named Kevin, Ann, Joe, Henry, or Maryann. The characters have been fictionalized for their privacy and my own.

I've described the region and the apartment complex in various, sometimes conflicting ways, to conceal the real location.

Incidents that seemed to be abuse or neglect are *exactly* what I observed on those dates, at those times, precisely as described.

To be very clear: I never saw Ann — or anyone else — actually *hit* Kevin. However, I heard her threaten to hit and beat him. I'm almost certain it was her voice I heard in Kevin's bedroom when I also heard the sound of slaps, thuds, and Kevin's screams.

I heard Kevin shouting things like, "Don't hit me, Momma!" many times during the year that they were my neighbors. I saw Kevin's swollen eyes, sometimes with bruises near them, as well as bruises on his arms and legs.

From what I heard, it seemed like Ann was beating her son at night after Joe went to bed. It sounded as if she was beating Kevin during the day, as well, when Joe wasn't at home.

But... what if I'm *wrong?*

Maybe Joe was the main abuser.

Joe's role in this has never been clear to me. I can't rule out his involvement in Kevin's problems. That's needs to be professionally evaluated.

Not hearing Joe's voice only means his voice is soft. After all, I could barely hear him when I was talking with him, in the hallway. He may have been abusing Kevin in a room that I couldn't hear clearly. I can't be sure. The only sounds that carried clearly were from rooms that adjoined ours.

Maybe Kevin wasn't physically abused. I have difficulty believing that, but he *might* have been doing some or all of the hitting, himself, while Ann was in his room. His grandmother suggested that might be part of the problem.

If so, this situation still needed immediate attention.

I tried to get help for Kevin. The police visited our apartment building when I called them. Usually, they knocked on Ann's door and went inside.

Afterward, the police told me they interviewed Ann, questioned Kevin, and checked him for cuts or bruises. They couldn't find enough evidence to remove Kevin from the home or file any charges.

Sometimes, it seemed like the police only *listened* outside Kevin's apartment. I'm not sure if they talked with Ann during those visits. Usually, I went back to bed. If the police couldn't hear anything to indicate a problem in Kevin's apartment, I understand why they'd have left. Nobody wants to wake a sleeping family without a good reason.

I think DHHS visited a few times. Other than that, I saw no active assessment — and certainly no improvements — in Kevin's home situation.

Mostly, I felt a complete lack of support from anyone close enough to Kevin to help him.

I want to believe Kevin's story was an extreme example. I want to think that, in most cases, neighbors and relatives *do* get involved.

However, the more I research this and talk with people about child abuse, the more I think Kevin's case wasn't just average, *it was better than most.*

That's chilling.

To Report Child Abuse or Neglect in NH

To contact the office of the NH Department of Health & Humans Services, Child Protective Services, contact 800-894-5533 (in state only), or 603-271-6562 (out of state) 8:00 AM. to 4:30 PM, Monday thru Friday. That reaches the intake office of the Division of Children, Youth, and Families.

However, as of 2012, it said at their webpage (http://www.dhhs.state.nh.us/dcyf/cps/index.htm), "DCYF receives more than 15,000 reports of suspected child abuse and neglect annually... Approximately 8,000 reports are assessed annually in NH."

In other words, slightly more than 50% of reported cases of abuse are assessed each year.

If your report is one of approximately *7,000 that aren't assessed,* you're not alone in your frustration. Continue to report the situation. With increased reports, the odds improve so the abused and/or neglected child has a better chance of receiving help.

Meanwhile, start looking for — or build — a local support system to prevent child abuse and neglect, and help families who aren't able to cope. In fact, every community should have several systems working together, including faith-based outreach when abuse or neglect are suspected.

The existing state system is overburdened. Shifting even more responsibility and blame onto them is not helpful. Help is more likely to come from people we know and see every day, for people we know and see every day.

In a 2007 statewide survey of victims of abuse, more than 70% of NH men reported a history that

includes physical assault
(http://www.nhcadsv.org/uploads/VAM
%20Report%20Final.pdf).

That's higher than the national average.

Among males who'd been physically assaulted, 34% of the perpetrators were women.

Those numbers surprised me. I thought I knew a lot about child abuse and neglect, but I didn't. Greater awareness can help individuals better recognize family problems when they see them.

Preventing child abuse and neglect isn't someone else's problem. It's rarely an issue that can be fully resolved by one person... not you, not me, and not someone with a desk and a title. That's especially true when his or her office is understaffed, underpaid, given limited latitude to take action, and overloaded with cases.

However, none of us can look the other way. As individuals, if we each do a little — as much as we can without compromising the time we need for our own families — we can make a difference.

Kevin's case was not unique. Chances are, you know a family in distress or a child who is being abused. I hope this book inspires action on your part, to protect the Kevins in your community, and make sure systems exist to help families trapped in patterns of abuse.

Shannon Bowen is a devoted wife, and the mother of three wonderful children. She's also a travel writer, and she's active with her church.

Her other book about Kevin is called *Momma, Stop! I'll Be Good!*

(That book, plus this one, are combined in the two-book set, *What Happened to Kevin.*)

With a friend, she co-authored *The Wicked Widow*, a story of marital betrayal.

You can contact Shannon at her website, Shannon-Bowen.com.

Love this book? Hated it? Have very mixed feelings?

Share your opinions at Amazon.com or the website where you learned about this book.

Tell others about this subject, too. It's important.

Thank you!

Made in the USA
Lexington, KY
22 March 2017